HOOKING UP
OR HOLDING
OUT

The Smart Girl's Guide to Driving Men Crazy and/or Finding True Love

Jamie Callan

SOURCEBOOKS CASABLANCA™

Published by Sourcebooks Casablanca, and imprint of Sourcebooks, Inc.
P.O. Box 4410, Naperville, Illinois 60567–4410
(630) 961–3900
FAX: (630) 961–2168
www.sourcebooks.com

Library of Congress Cataloging-in-Publication Data

Callan, Jamie.
  Hooking up or holding out : the smart girl's guide to driving men
crazy and/or finding true love / Jamie Callan.
       p. cm.
  Includes bibliographical references.
  ISBN-13: 978-1-4022-0820-1 (alk. paper)
  ISBN-10: 1-4022-0820-0 (alk. paper)
  1. Man-woman relationships. 2. Dating (Social customs) 3. Mate
selection. I. Title.

HQ801.C269 2006
646.7'7--dc22

2005019881

Printed and bound in the United States of America
DR 10 9 8 7 6 5 4 3 2 1

For my Dad,
an Officer and a Gentleman

Foreword

> As all those who write about civic matters show and all history proves by a multitude of examples, whoever organizes a state and establishes its laws must assume that all men are wicked and will act wickedly whenever they have the chance to do so. He must also assume that whenever their wickedness remains hidden for a time there is a hidden reason for it which remains unknown for want of occasion to make it manifest. But time, which is called the father of all truth, uncovers it.
>
> —from *The Prince* by Niccolo Machiavelli

This is a revolutionary book for women. It's full of dangerous suggestions on fueling the flames of desire, longing, romance, and sexuality.

This is *not* a book about honest, open communication, working on understanding your mate, or the proper care and feeding of your boyfriend.

This is certainly not a book about rules.

This, in fact, is a book about breaking all the rules and really misbehaving. Read this book if you're ready to bring back fun, intrigue, and subterfuge into romance. Read it if you're ready for a delicious chase. Read this book if you're really ready and willing to take back the power of your sex.

You hold in your hands—right now—a roadmap for a brave new future. Now, take a deep breath and get ready for the new sexual revolution.

A Special Message to Men

Okay, so you're reading this book because you want to know what new tricks women have up their sleeves. You're nervous, a little tense. I understand this. Don't worry about it—it's natural. Besides, you're in good hands.

It's like this for you: during the sixties, life became a feast and you were happy. Women were supposedly equal. They wanted sex just as much as you did and they weren't coy about it, either. What a relief. No more games; just great sex whenever you felt like it.

Now, you're wondering—suppose all that slips away? Suppose all the women in the world are suddenly not so free and easy? Suppose they start playing those retro-1950s no sex—I'm keeping my virginity—I have a headache—I'm really in love with Roger—type games? What will happen then? Damn!

Okay, calm down. It's actually not as bad as it sounds. I know what I'm doing here. And I'm doing it because I love men. I love men a lot. In fact, I think about you all the time and I like to think up new ways to torture you. Just kidding. Actually, maybe not. But, here's the good news—I am completely invested in the idea of making sex and love and romance interesting, artful, and a whole lot more fun.

It's like this—when you play baseball, or try to catch the illusive blue fish, or calculate a move in a game of chess—or even when you buy into that tech stock before it shoots through the roof—don't you feel great? And it's not about actually catching the pop fly, the blue fish, checkmate, or making a killing on Wall Street. It's about getting there. It's about using your brains and brawn to outwit your rivals. This adds heat. And this is what you want in your relationships with women: heat. Lots of heat.

But here's the problem, guys. You're like that old snake sitting in the reptile cage at the San Diego Zoo. Every now and then, the zookeeper comes by and throws a frozen mouse that's been barely thawed into your cage. You lazily look up, open one eye, and regretfully swallow the thing whole. It tastes like tissue and you hate yourself. You hate your life. You hate the goddamn dead mouse and you hate the people gawking at you through the glass partition.

Dear snake, old snake—I am offering you something living. Something clever and smart and fun. I am offering you an equal partner in this game of love. I am offering you fresh live mice that you can chase. No, you're not going to catch us every time, but you're going to have a hell of a good time and you're going to feel alive! And I think that's better than a barely thawed TV mouse dinner any old day of the week.

So, gentlemen—awake. Open your eyes. Get up and get out of your cages, because the chase begins here and now.

Contents

Fasten Your seat Belt, Baby

Admit it. You love that dark look in a man's eyes when he's just a little bit frustrated. He wants you badly and he'll do anything to get you. You love the way he pours on the sweet talk, his tongue practically hanging out of his mouth as he buys you another drink and admires your eyes, your mouth, your cleavage. You love the way he promises you the moon. You love the little tricks he plays to get closer—accidentally on purpose rubbing his arm against your arm. You relish the moment he throws caution to the wind, and despite all the risks, he goes for broke and leans over and kisses you full on the mouth, without hesitation, without permission, completely aware that he may get a hard slap across the face. But, he does it anyway, because you've driven him crazy.

Let's face it. Men love the chase. They love beating out the competition. They're completely goal driven, and more than anything else in the world, they're driven by the goal of sex. No, they're not driven by the desire to obtain money or fame or power. They're not driven by a need to be admired and appreciated for their good deeds and altruism. No, they're driven by their need for sex. They only want money and fame and power and adoration because they think it'll help them get more sex!

And the cold, hard fact is that once they have their sexual needs met and they're completely satisfied and satiated—they pay less attention. They drift. They lose focus. They aren't in the mood for courtship, long walks in the park, or holding your hand under a moonlit sky. You can forget about that. Look at it this way—after sex, it's like they've got a belly-full of Dinty Moore Beef Stew and they just don't feel like getting up and going for a run around the block (read: talking, complimenting, cuddling, romancing, buying little trinkets, and paying attention to us)! So, what's the answer? How do we get men to sit up and focus? To notice us, to call, to come back, to court, to woo, to listen, to love, adore, cherish, and take us to Block Island for the weekend? The answer is simple and yet deeply complicated. We must revolt against the system.

Let's Misbehave

Consider contemporary film and literature—from *Fight Club* to *The Human Stain*, from *Bridget Jones's Diary* to both versions of *The Thomas Crown Affair*. Think of all those fabulous old black and white movies. Ginger Rogers and Fred Astaire. Katharine Hepburn infuriating Spencer Tracy in *Woman of the Year*. Marlene Dietrich driving the professor crazy in *The Blue Angel*. Each one of the heroines in these books and films is very different, but they were all hot. Why? Because they were unpredictable. They misbehaved. They were emotional. They had messy lives. They were not compliant or easy. They offered resistance.

Don't we think of a man's enduring a woman's difficult nature as a sign that he's in it for the long term, that he really loves her, that he understands her? In literature and film, we want the guy to fight to get the girl, to deserve the girl—why shouldn't we want the same in our own lives?

The problem is, we've bent over backward to make things easy for men, to please them. We love sex, we love love, we love romance, we love men—we love them all so much that we've taken the reins of courtship away from them and done all the pursuing—and along the way sometimes completely missing and then running over some very nice, sincere—perhaps shy—guys.

We ask—well, why can't women just go out and ask for what they want? Why can't we just be pals with men? Why can't we be perfectly honest with them? After all, don't men like gals who are easy to get along with; low-maintenance sweetie-pies? Dependable. Fun. Not too demanding. Good in bed. Eager to please.

No! That's nonsense and besides it's no fun—it's boring! You've seen it—men who leave perfectly lovely women for the most unlikely, inappropriate, seemingly incompatible gal imaginable. Why do they do this? Because men get unhappy and complacent if the woman in their life is predictable. Truth is, men want women who are a little difficult. They'll deny it, but you see it over and over again—men who stray from great girlfriends/wives/lovers. Why do they do it? The answer is simple: men love the adventure, the resistance, the struggle, the victory. They love whatever it is they don't have. They want to fight the good fight and win the fair maiden. Or they want to tame the shrewish bitch from the wrong side of town. Or the coy kitten from Connecticut. The waif with the learning disability. The gal with the mysterious past. The woman from Algiers. The fatal-attraction chick, the mysterious girl from Bali, the beauty from Japan, the woman who's married to their best friend, the wacky art student from Kansas, the actress in that shampoo commercial.

Men want to be shaken out of their rut. They want to feel alive. They want a change. They want to be stimulated. They want something new.

What do these women have in common? First of all and most important, they're different from who the man is with now. They may also be elusive or unattainable, or they're volatile or crazy or "strange" or just plain figments of their imagination. They all offer resistance. They might be difficult to capture, or a dangerous fling, or they present the possibility of truly upending a man's life. Sometimes, these women are just out of reach, and yet enticingly within reach. They represent an imaginary landscape that is full of possibility. Greener pastures. Next year's model. The bigger and better supercharged thing with a zillion hopped-up megahertz that only really, really macho guys are hep to. Yes, all that—and oh, yes…rapture.

What can you do in the face of such a seemingly impossible situation? How can you be the object of a man's obsession? Actually, it's relatively easy. It's a matter of being truly challenging—because you challenge yourself. When you shake yourself out of a rut and demand new things of yourself, you not only feel strong and entitled and empowered, but hey, you also attract hot guys!

This might mean that you're a little unpredictable or mysterious or difficult. It definitely means giving up the notion once and for all that you should always give men everything they desire. It means that you can't always be perfectly honest with men. It doesn't mean that you're not nice or kind or sweet or flirtatious, but it does mean that you are not going to be so easily forthcoming in your physical affections. You offer resistance. It means playing the field, and always being on the lookout for a new fella to add to your retinue of admirers—even after you've been married for fifty years.

The Art of Love

To truly change the system, you will begin by taking the art of romance seriously. You will consciously create a plan of seduction and strategize your every move for maximum effect. You'll have to start thinking of yourself as the heroine in your own novel and the star of your own movie. You're going to have to be a little secretive, a bit of a flirt, a naughty girl, a regular coquette. You're going to make a man wait an excruciatingly long time before you deign to grant him your sexual favors. You're going to learn how to flirt, when to be forthcoming in your affections, when to withhold them. You'll practice your art on a daily basis. You'll see every man you encounter as an opportunity to try out your skills. You'll slow down the process of love, so that it can be truly appreciated and savored. On your road trip to romance, you're going to get off the superhighway of sex and take the back roads.

Ready for all that? Then climb aboard, fasten your seat belts, and get ready.

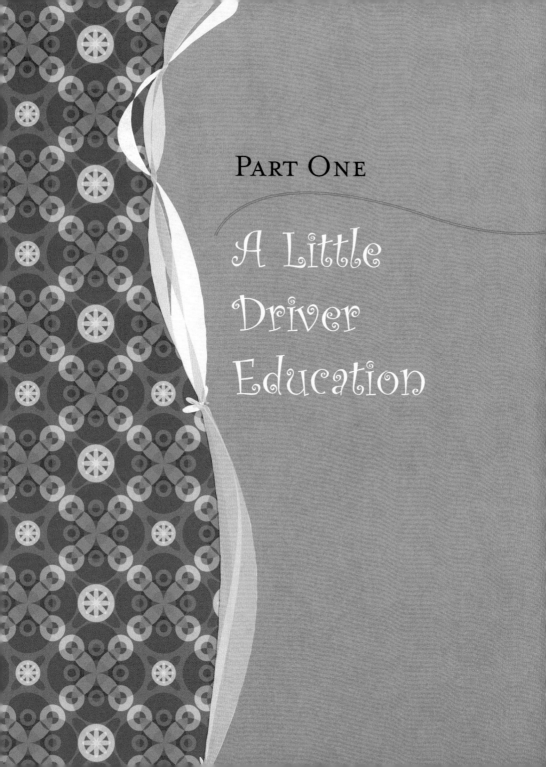

Part One

A Little Driver Education

chapter one

Love Is Not a Freeway

The problem with love in the fast lane

> Women blame men for acting fake...But women are the ones speeding from zero to intimacy like a Ferrari. Which is more artificial?
>
> —from Rick Marin's memoir,
> *Cad: Confessions of a Toxic Bachelor*

Men want sex and we want sex. And perhaps we want sex even more than men. The truth is we can go on for hours and hours and days and days of marathon sex. We really love sex, lots of sex and love and sex and well, we all really love undivided attention from the right man. We love his desire, his focus. Just as men say they are visual creatures and they cannot help themselves when they ogle women, the truth is we love it when a man really sees us and works at pleasing us. We love men who truly pay close attention to our needs and desires. We like a man who notices what we're wearing and the color of our hair. We thrive on the male gaze.

And men thrive on visual stimulation. So, how do we get a man to focus in on one woman—you and only you?

Consider what drives a man. Well, sex, of course and if not that, then how about sex? Or maybe some sexual sublimation—food or beer or making money or racecar driving or beating his best friend at squash.

But basically, here's what he wants: to have sex with you.

You're Complicated. You Want More.

Here's what you want: to be courted, adored, wooed, admired, listened to, understood, wooed some more, forgiven for your foibles, your little peccadilloes, chased, called, pleaded with, cared for, kissed, loved, loved, loved—and to have great sex.

You see the problem here? We want more stuff than they want. We want courtship. Not only that, but we want to be courted artfully. We want to have fun, to take things slowly, to make them last. We want a courtship that gives us the opportunity to wear great clothes, eat in nice restaurants, travel, dance, go to theatre and movies and sports events, and weekends in the country. Some of us want a man who'll buy us trinkets or help our career, impress our friends, keep us company on rainy days in front of the fireplace. Some of us want love and marriage or a perhaps a man who'll kill all our enemies (in a humane way, of course).

You see, we want a lot. So, how do we make sure we get everything we want in addition to the sex that all of us want? Very simply—make sure we get all the courting before we have sex.

It sounds like a good idea in theory, but I know what you're thinking—I need a lot of courting, wooing, admiration, love, etc., and no man is going to wait for sex until I get my fill! I'm not diminishing this problem. It's really a problem. Men have become very spoiled, because the truth is, if a man really wants sex, well, he can, with a little effort, go out there and find a woman who's willing to have sex with him. He'll probably have to buy her dinner and a drink, be relatively nice and tell her she's really attractive a few times before hitting the sack. And if that doesn't work, there are a lot of books on the market to help men through the process of seducing women—from creating a "harem" (from *How to Succeed with Women*) to cultivating "the good-for-now girl" (from *What Men Want*) to how to get a girl into bed quickly and then why he should get rid of her within a month so she doesn't think he's her boyfriend.

Men know what they're doing. They'll deny it, but they practice the art of quick seduction, deception, and betrayal on a daily basis. It's the old "catch and release" method of courtship. And men have been having a field day with it since the dawn of the so-called Sexual Revolution. So many women, so little time, they are thinking. And imagine, without the tyranny of a biological clock ticking, they can spend a good twenty to thirty years bedding as many babes as humanly possible before settling down in middle-age with a nice twenty-something girl. Bastards!

But, this is reality, so let's face it head on.

A Little History Lesson

Here's a little history. Imagine this scenario—one day in 1968, some clever, highly manipulative fellas looked at the women's movement and the introduction of the birth-control pill, along with our declarations that we wanted to be treated equally and said—hey, I can use this to get more chicks to go to bed with me! Just imagine it for a moment—a little cabal of hippie guys meets one hot August night in Taos, New Mexico, by the commune swimming hole and decide that equal rights for women is a great idea if it means women will shag lots of guys and enjoy sex the way men enjoy sex. They came up with a great brand name for it too—the Sexual Revolution. It sounds very cool, doesn't it? Very liberating and exciting and new. And so began the era of Free Love. (As if love could ever possibly come without some kind of a price.)

But, the truth is, it's the oldest ploy in the book.

And we totally bought into it! You know why? Because men are much better at this social/sexual game playing than we are! They've been doing it since they got out of the womb. They love sports. They love strategy. They love closing the deal. They do it in their sleep. They don't even know they're doing it! But when we play games—oh, it's shocking and terrible. Why? Because we're so bad at it, they see right through our manipulations. The answer is not honesty, because we could be honest with men, but men will never be honest with us.

Well, actually they are occasionally honest with us—look at *The Man Show*. This was a show on Comedy Central featuring two schlubby guys, hooting at a posse of big-busted gals called "The Juggies." At the end of every show they feature girls in very short (often pleated, sometimes plaid) skirts jumping on trampolines, all filmed in slow motion so the men can get a good gander at legs, buttocks, and cotton panties, while they chug beer, burp, and drool. This is a man being honest. Not a pretty picture. This is probably why they see the need to play games with us. If only we knew the whole truth, would we really be so quick to shed our clothes?

True, all men are not like these guys. Some men are sweet and sexy and handsome and loving and serious and funny and regular princes. They just want the same things we want—love and courtship and travel and walks along the beach at sunset and oh yeah, sex. First and foremost, sex.

And the truth is, we want sex too. We love men and we need sex. Lots and lots of sex. We're lusty women. We are loving women. We love sex and we love men and yeah, we love great sex. Unfortunately, if they know that we want sex just as much as they do, perhaps more—and we go ahead and satisfy these desires, theirs and ours with no struggle—then what leverage do we have left when we wake up the next morning, vaguely unsatisfied, and hungry for more—more hugs, more compliments, more attention, more romance, more conversation, more time together, more shopping sprees, more trips to the country?

That's when the man is tired! He doesn't want to hear about our needs. He doesn't want to buy us trinkets or compliment us or listen to the difficulties we're having with our Internet provider. He doesn't want to smile and nod and offer compliments. He does those things to get sex. We gave him the sex. Now he wants to go home, have a beer, watch some bad TV, and take a snooze.

Simply put, he's after sex, but you're after sex and love. What can you do?

Make him wait. Make getting you into bed difficult—the first time, the third time, the seventeenth time, and the fifty-seven thousandth time. Getting you into bed should always demand a bit of art both on your part and on his. It should be an exquisitely intricate dance. Never let him take it for granted.

Oh, and once he gets you into bed, and he thinks he's got you figured out, change the lock and combination immediately. He should never believe he's got you figured out. This will certainly slow things down. And that's what you want.

Consider what we're dealing with here. Listen to the way men talk about us. They love the sport of dating. It's a wonderful game for them. They are basically trying to bed as many women as possible before allowing themselves "to get caught" by a nice gal.

Case History of a Cad

In his memoir, *Cad: Confessions of a Toxic Bachelor*, Rick Marin offers up an extremely entertaining wake-up call. He went through women the way we go through shoes. How could he manage it? Well, first Rick tells us how he plies them with drinks, a few compliments, mistily reveals his failed first marriage, removes his eyeglasses, and gives the gals a soulful stare. Next thing you know, he is waking up with the blinding morning sun in his eyes, and when he sees there's this strange chick in his bed, he wants her out. Now. Immediately! This goes on and on for Rick until one day he meets Ilene. She's the only one who doesn't hop into bed with him. She's difficult. She's always surrounded by a coterie of adoring men. She's gorgeous, but she's "not dating" right now. She forces him to take long drives on the Long Island Expressway. She runs hot and cold. She makes fun of him in public and apologizes profusely (and prettily) in private. She's a busy gal. She's often around, but she's never really available. She rejects his advances and treats him like he's her "walker," meaning he walks her home and no more. So, what does Rick do?

He marries her!

I suggest you read this book like it's your own personal dating cabala.

While men might behave as if love is a sport, it's our job to slow them down and transform it into an art. You may ask why it's our job to slow them down. Why can't the guys do their part to put on the brakes?

Why should they? For them, there's very little consequence to moving in quickly and getting out just as quickly. Plus, what red-blooded guy is going to get all sensitive and slow down and look at you teary-eyed and say, "Sweetheart, can we slow things down? You're really going too fast for me! I need to know—do you really care about me?" Do you honestly want to be with a guy like that, anyway? No, you want a guy who has some drive, a little oomph. His attempts at chasing you, pursuing you, seducing you are all signs that he's going for the distance. So, make him go a long distance. Make this race a marathon, not a sprint.

The Myth of the Sensitive Guy: The Birth of the Baby Man

Generally, if a guy's engine isn't revving from the get-go, he lacks stamina, strength, and interest. He's probably conflicted or he's a Wimpster (see Rachel Elder's excellent article "What Up, Wimpster?" in the summer 2004 issue of *Bust* magazine) or perhaps he's just not available to you right now. Perhaps he's actually married. Sometimes the guy with the stalled motor is sincerely shy or wounded or incredibly cautious for various reasons. This still doesn't mean you should be the one to hit the gas. That's only asking for a crash, because the problem is, a man has no brake mechanism. He'll let you do all the work—the pursuit, the phone calls, pay for dinner and shag him, and then he'll call you on the phone one night and say, "Gee wiz, I forgot to tell you—I'm still in love with my ex-girlfriend. That's right, she lives in Cincinnati and she's married and we haven't talked in four years, but I just can't get her out of my mind and I don't want to lead you on and hurt you." This declaration comes after he's had three months of great sex.

And let's say he honestly isn't ready to pursue you. Let's say he's going back to school, recovering from a divorce, repairing his finances, figuring out just who he really is, etc., and he's not equipped to pursue you. To stretch a metaphor, he's in the repair shop, he needs a tune-up, maybe a new carburetor. Leave him be. You don't want to be with a guy who's going to need road assistance in the middle of a rainy night because he's broken down on the side of the highway once again.

And finally, here's a scientific explanation for why it's good to give men some resistance. It's just logical that when a man pushes things forward while the woman pulls them back you create movement. This makes the man work at getting you—and out of that effort you get friction, drama, drive, power, romance, sexual tension, and plenty of heat. It's thermodynamic. You need the push and pull. It's what puts the steam in sex, baby.

Women of the World Unite!

If we work together as women in a concerted effort, we can restructure a dating system that's gone to the dogs. Let's start by slowing things down and holding back a little. Let's show men an air of being unattainable. This will not dampen their spirits but inflame them. No man truly values something that is easily or effortlessly attained. No, both men and women value the thing that is just out of reach, that is beautiful, achingly charming, and coveted by others. Think of an exclusive restaurant or a rare wine or a hard-to-reach holiday destination. It is the fine, rare thing that man cannot get without patience, effort, longing, and competition that fuels the flames of his desire.

Why should you wait for sex, if all you really want is sex? Why create an air of mystery and unavailability? Why create a sense of competition and exclusivity? We're all modern women. Why not just have sex when the mood strikes? Well, it may be true that a quick roll in the hay can have its charms, but after a while—say a dozen quick rolls in the hay with a dozen different men (or cads, really) one grows weary and maybe even slightly annoyed and sore from all those prickly things that are found in piles of hay. Ultimately, it's not all that much fun. This kind of sex, especially when repeated over and over again with guys who come and go, leaves a gal feeling a little dissatisfied. Of course it's our right to have sex as much as we want, to own our own sexuality, to be in charge of our own bodies. This is what our grandmothers and mothers and we have fought for and we are still fighting for—but have we truly been thinking of our own interests?

Here's the flaw in this notion of equal sexual opportunity—women do not enjoy sex the same way men enjoy sex. Of course this is no surprise. But why is it we bought into the fantasy that if only we were free enough we could enjoy sex in the same way men enjoy it? This is a pretty ridiculous notion, because the fact is, we generally enjoy sex more than men. Just get out that old Edith Hamilton paperback on Greek mythology and look up Tiresias. To settle an argument between Zeus and Hera on who enjoys sex more—man or woman—Tiresias transforms himself first into a mortal man to have sex, then a mortal woman. He tells Zeus and Hera that women absolutely, inequitably, enjoy sex more than men!

And isn't it really true? So why would you want to be like a man? Why not enjoy sex as a woman? What does this mean? Well, you like to take your time; that for you, there's an emotional element to good lovemaking; that you're less linear and more circuitous than a male. You're less interested in the Aristotelian thrust of inciting incident, followed by rapidly building tension directed into a climax and then falling quickly into resolution (read: sleep). No, you like a more circular coming and going, a tantric kind of lovemaking that knows no beginning and no end, but just keeps going and going and going and going.

And this scares men!

The Truth about Cave Men

This is why they get nervous and look around for something else, something new—it's because they can never give us enough and they know it. That's why they have to crawl into their "caves" every now and then, as John Gray explains in *Men Are from Mars, Women Are from Venus*. During this fragile post-sex spent state, men are in a refractory condition and they descend rapidly into their flight mode. If you've had sex with a man whom you don't really know and you have very little time or experience invested together, and if he has never had to court you, wait an excruciating long time to bed you, or fight off competition, this flight will be more than just a temporary sojourn into his nearby cave. He'll run to a cave in another time zone where you probably won't hear from him again until the next time he's desperately in need of sex. Not your company, not your pretty smile, not your amazing mind or sparkling personality, but your sex. This is what he wants. This is what drives him—at least until he actually gets to know you as a real human being. But this is never going to happen if he never gets to know you outside of a sexual context and he's certainly not going to really get to know you after three dates.

So, what do you do?

First, slow him down. How do you do this? Well, not by being easy and giving him whatever he wants, whenever he wants it. If he gives up on you because you're not having sex right away, then forget him. He wasn't in it for the long-term. He has no vision, no artfulness; he doesn't know anything about courtship or seduction; he has no patience and no imagination. And he's probably still in love with that gal in Cincinnati. Good riddance.

He can't Buy Your Love

Make him wait. Let months go by. Let him be a cad, just like Rick Marin, and get his bad-boy ways out of his system, just not with you. If you're dating and he's laying out big bucks to impress you and this is making you uncomfortable, put a stop to it. Don't fall for the high-pressure sale. Rather, keep him at bay. Don't let him distract you with shiny objects and expensive dinners. Hold out for as long as possible. Cool down the sexual pressure. Don't ever go to his apartment late at night or let him into your place alone. Men take this as a signal that the coast is clear. Keep things light. Fun. Flirt, but be mysterious, and most important, make the scene. He needs to see that there is competition for your company, so show yourself off. Go to parties and events where lots of fellas can vie for your attention. Try to arrange it so that he is witness to the power of your charms. Let him see you doing what you do best—whether it's playing the piano or making your own sushi or volunteering at a homeless shelter—he should see you as a force in the world. He should realize you are respected, accomplished, loved, adored, and surrounded by other men.

The reason I suggest this is not because of some feminist manifesto, but rather, in this instance, for a much less idealistic reason. A guy is going to be very careful with a woman who is a part of a community, is respected, accomplished, and connected. He'll have more at stake if he knows he is being "watched" and he'll try harder to please her.

You can be affectionate and flirtatious, but stay away from overt sexual innuendos. He'll try to subtly bring the subject of sex into conversations. Steer clear. He should be kept in the dark regarding your true intentions. Be polite, appropriate, sweet, sexy, but not sexual. Keep him guessing.

After a while, you can start giving him little treats. You can kiss, touch, hug, etc. Just no getting naked for a long time. He's going to get frustrated and a man who's frustrated is much more creative, much more willing to work hard at getting want he wants. A man who is frustrated will be a tremendous lover when the time comes. He will be determined and very, very excited. And most important, a man who's been made to wait will have more invested in the relationship (time, money, strategies, mutual friendships, his secrets, your secrets). And in the long term, he'll be less likely to throw you over on a whim. Plus, it'll give you the chance to discover what he's really like and whether you really want to be with this man. Why waste your time driving in the wrong direction for miles and miles? Why waste your energy on a guy who just wants a quick sexual fix and then to be on his way? Why allow yourself to be taken out of social circulation by a guy who isn't up to snuff?

No, the interview process should take place outside the bedroom when your heads are clear.

Make Breaking up Hard to Do

Here's the other advantage to making him wait. After months of dating, you're in a relationship. There's no denying it. Even the books on seducing women tell the guys that after six weeks, they're in a relationship and it's much harder to bail. In *How to Succeed with Women*, Ron Louis and David

Copeland explain, "One of the hardest parts of being a successful seducer is the break-up process." They suggest men not date a woman for more than a month because, well, after a month things begin to get serious. It makes the breakup harder to do and things get complicated. You get to know each other's friends and families. If the man is a hit-and-run driver, after a month there's bound to be witnesses to the crime. So if you get to know him and he goes to parties and shows and events with you and meets your friends and family, then he's much less likely to see you as his next victim. He's not going to bulldoze you into a compromising position and then take off, knowing there is no one around to call him on his dastardly ways.

Think of it—has any man ever regretted the fact that you made him wait? No. They secretly love it—it's sexy. It's titillating. It's foreplay. It's the thrill of the chase. Men only get annoyed with waiting when they want drive-thru sex. Easy in. Easy out. And who wants fast-food sex? It's cheap and greasy and leaves you feeling bloated the next day.

You may say—"but I can't fall in love with a man until I've had sex with him. It's the good sex that really hooks me." So? What's so great about getting hooked on a guy who's good in bed and bad in life? Just because a man is a good lover doesn't mean he's going to treat you well outside the bedroom. It doesn't even mean he's going to be around very long. And you have to wonder—why is he so good at having sex with a gal he really hardly knows? Maybe he does this sort of thing a lot.

And consider those guys who actually are very good lovers but are just not capable of having sex with a virtual stranger. These fellas are often the ones who are the most artful lovers because they integrate intimacy, emotion, and love into the sex right from the get-go because they've taken the time—and sometimes a long time—to form a foundation of friendship first. But, if you are being tied up (perhaps literally) by a Casanova, then there's a very good chance you won't even be around to notice when the real deal comes along.

During this waiting period, date other guys. Keep lots of eggs in your basket. And if there's one man whom you really do care for, then you can use this platonic phase to really consider whether you want to be intimate with him. It's a great opportunity to see how well he does in the courtship arena. Is he seductive, playful, creative, patient? Or does he lose his temper, act like a jerk, and sulk? It's good to find out these things before you let him get too close. This sounds like common sense, but you'd be surprised how many women offer their sexual favors to men who seem lovely during the first three dates and then quickly turn into jerks.

There is an art to love and sex. It can be beautiful, passionate, upsetting, emotional, intelligent, thought-provoking, and delicious—if you're willing to take your time.

The End of the Instant Girlfriend and Fast-Food Love

Treat courtship and love as high art; not a game, not a contest, but rather, an art. A theatrical production. Something shapely and beautiful. A gourmet meal prepared with love, tenderness, and intelligence, rather than fast-food garbage, a lousy sitcom, a paint-by-numbers painting, or an unrehearsed dance where no one bothered to consider lighting or costume or took the time to practice and get to actually know the movements and rhythms and styles of their dance partners. If the concepts of love and courtship are elevated to art, then sex will not be some messy, confused thing that happens in the heat of the moment and you regret the next morning when you lie there in bed among the gnarled sheets, trying to remember the name of the guy who flung the pair of SpongeBob SquarePants boxers on top of your dresser.

We've always known that when it comes to sex and romance, women are in the driver's seat, but for some strange/crazy reason, we gave the wheel over to the guys, and you known what? They're reckless drivers. They're speed demons. They have absolutely no sense of driver courtesy. Girls, it's time to take back control.

chapter two

What Drives Men?

Sex. And if not that—how about sex? And of course, there's always sex!

> "As men, we love the conquest. We love the accomplishment of taking this woman who at first seemed like an impossibility and knowing that we now 'have her.'
>
> —from Ron Louis and David Copeland's
> *How to Succeed with Women*

Just listen to them. Watch the movies they produce, the television series they write, the books they write and review. Listen to them give speeches. Go to their comedy shows. Eavesdrop on their conversations. Just ask them. The male point of view is no big secret. They are completely guileless when it comes to letting their needs and wants be known. We just don't want to believe what we hear is true. We're so damn naive, we are always trying to figure out what's really going on beneath the surface. What childhood traumas or societal pressures may have caused the man to be such a snake.

And even if they say, "No, we're not snakes. We're wussies! We're sensitive. We're misunderstood! Why, we're pussywhipped!" Don't believe them, they're just saying this to get into your panties.

Why? Because they're snakes! And even if they're not, they are!

It's All in the Research, Baby

Do the research. Listen to what the authors of *What Men Want: Three Professional Single Men Reveal to Women What It Takes to Make a Man Yours* by

Bradley Gerstman, Esq., Christopher Pizzo, CPA, and Rich Seldes, MD (a lawyer, a certified public accountant, and a doctor, ladies!) would like women to know about them:

1. They get bored easily. This is part of their anatomical structure. The poor creatures can't help it. They get excited, hard, harder, they come, and then they want to run away or go to sleep. They don't like to be seen or touched in this spent state. It makes them feel vulnerable. One way for them to avoid feeling vulnerable is to get out while the going is good and find some new women. And if they can't do that, then how about hanging out at the strip joint with their buddies?

2. Men like variety. Fidelity is really difficult for them. Again, this is because they feel vulnerable after a sexual liaison, and they have a really hard time integrating sex with friendship. As regressive as it sounds, men generally think of sex as "dirty" and something you do with "dirty" girls, and when they wake up the next morning and remember that they're not really with a "dirty" girl, but a very nice girl (unless you actually are a "dirty" girl), they panic. They feel guilty and they want a new girl they can "defile."

3. Men worship their penis. They see their penis as a magical sword. They can knock down castle walls, conquer the enemy, and force their will upon a fair maiden—all with their magical penis sword!

The Magical Penis

Honestly, this last part is true for men—no matter how old they are and how many years they've had to become accustomed to the magical workings of their penis, it is still amazing. And yes, they think of themselves as knights in shining armor. And as cliché as this may sound, a man likes to think of you as the virgin maiden. He's the only one who's ever slept with you. And barring that, he's the first one to awaken your sexuality. Lots of men may want you, but only he has been strong enough and brave enough to win you over.

And if you're not the virgin bride, then you're the monster demon whore from hell. Or the simple slut from the wrong side of town. Or maybe the little harlot with the heart of gold. Or the tramp, the floozy, the tart, and so on and so forth. It's hard to believe all the names they've got for a sexual woman. It's all so black and white. This is because a man simply doesn't trust a woman who's truly sexual. It really scares him. This is because he's really insecure, because he is well aware of the limitations of his magical penis. He knows that what goes up, must come down. He knows that there are days when it is not so magical, after all. He knows that all men have magical penises. And some men's magical penises are bigger or better than his magical penis. And then there's the deep-down Freudian memory of comparing his little-boy penis with his daddy's big, grownup penis, and the sudden realization that he's never going to truly wrest mommy's attention away from such a stunning specimen of manhood.

Okay, I've done a fair bit of editorializing here, and you won't find all this in the *What Men Want*, but the truth is that all this really makes a man nervous. He does not like to think that maybe you've seen a few magical penises that are actually bigger and better than his. He likes to believe that you think his penis is the greatest, most wonderful magical penis ever in the whole history of the universe. And the only way for him to convince himself that you truly think this is so is to tell himself (as ridiculous as this may seem) that you have never actually been with any other magical penises as amazing as his magical penis.

In *What Men Want*, the authors are completely honest and straightforward. They come right out and tell us what they want. Here it is boiled down to the essential facts (with very little editorializing on my part, honest).

Brace yourself.

1. Men divide women up into two categories—the "good-for-now girl"

(meaning good for sex) and the "good girl" they might marry if she is everything he wants and needs in a woman (and mother approves).

2. Men like girls they might marry to cook homemade meals for them.
3. Men also like these girls to make their beds after a sleepover and to pick up around the house.
4. Men like fellatio.
5. Men will tolerate cunnilingus, but make sure you're "clean" and "well-groomed."
6. Men like lots of fellatio.
7. Men like variety.
8. Men like lingerie.
9. Men like women who don't talk too much about their lives.
10. Men like women who listen to *them* talk about *their* lives.
11. Men like fellatio and "don't stop until he's finished."
12. Men cheat on women they supposedly love (but that's only because "men have these desires eating at them all the time").
13. Men don't like it when you make them feel jealous. (But don't you dare get jealous when they ogle the waitress—after all, they have those desires eating at them all the time!)
14. Men don't really want to get married.
15. Men like hot-looking women.
16. Men like lots of sex (especially fellatio)!
17. Men don't like to talk about sex; they like to have sex.
18. Men like women to smile at them, encourage conversation, flirt, give them their telephone number, touch them gently but seductively to signal their receptivity, be home when they do call, be really nice on the first date, listen to them, don't talk too much about anything meaningful, and call them after the first date to reassure them that it

was wonderful (unless he didn't really like you very much—in which case, please don't ever call him).

19. Men like it when you buy them presents.
20. Men like fellatio, but if that gets boring, they like anal sex.

Okay, are you completely appalled? Don't be. These are three ordinary guys just trying to be honest. There's very little subterfuge here. In a way, it's refreshing.

Rather than getting annoyed, think of ways you can use this information to drive men crazy. Consider the notion of the "good girl" and the "good-for-now girl." What exactly does this mean? Simply this; a guy will play the field, sleep with as many women as possible, enjoy the scenery, until one day he'll settle down with a "good girl." According to our professional men, a good girl is not as quick to "put out" as the "good-for-now girl." A good girl gets along with his mama, cooks, buys him gifts, and caters to his needs. She's not the one with all the sex toys who just dropped in from Paris for the weekend with a bottle of Veurve Clicquot and two hours to kill before she catches a flight to the Other Coast. That's the good-for-now girl. Very good for now, if you ask the guy. How can he refuse such a great opportunity?

Don't Waste the Calories

Honestly, sometimes it's fun for us to play the "good-for-now girl" and certainly we've been with men we consider "good-for-now guys," but ultimately, this game is full of empty calories and it's a distraction that takes us away from cultivating more suitable, more worthy admirers. Plus it's a terrible time waster. And as women, we don't have all that much time to waste. As harsh and even unfair as this sounds, our power to attract is tied up with our beauty and in this world at this moment in time, youth is beauty. Yes, brains are beautiful and talent is beautiful and money and success are all beautiful and powerful. But for a woman wanting to find true love at this moment in history, the power of her good looks is paramount. This isn't to say there's an expiration date on beauty or that this is the sole source of a woman's power. It's simply to say that as we age, our most potent resource in the dating world may diminish. So why waste time and beauty and youth on some shallow lad who only wants you to be his good-for-now girl?

And if you're interested in starting a family, consider the fact that our fertility does have an expiration date (although, in *Backlash*, Susan Faludi explains how this expiration date has been manipulated to scare women and get us so nervous that we'll marry any old schlub that comes along with good haircut and a bag full of seeds). Okay, I made that last part up, but consider the fact that men love thinking about their virtually limitless supply of sperm. They say things like "we have trouble being faithful because we have a need to spread our seed" (see *What Men Want*). They like to imagine all that sperm racing and swirling inside their bodies, anxious to speedily release itself upon the world, like some kind of sexed-up Johnny Appleseed.

It all seems quite unfair when you think about it—men running around nailing as many women as possible, in as short a time as possible, as if they were going for the gold in the Sex Olympics.

What's a gal to do? Well, we can stop giving them the trophy every other minute. We can make it more difficult for them to reach their goal and win the big prize. How? Well, consider the Grand Prix. Why do we care whether the guy in the blue car makes it to the finish line in five minutes or ten minutes? I'll tell you why—it's because the guy in the red car is trailing close behind him, and because the cowboy from Tennessee is pushing up to the lead. It's because the driver from Atlanta has just crashed into the sidelines. Because the old-timer in the yellow car is making a comeback. Because that maverick from New York City is threatening to upturn the whole race with an unexpected win.

The Thrill of the Chase

Men love competition, and admit it, you love to be fought over—artfully, of course. It may sound retro, but think about it—you know it's true. It's always been true, but men are not going to admit to the fact that seeing a woman who is surrounded by other admirers, laughing and flirting, is going to drive them wild with desire. But it will. This is because men are like hunting dogs.

Have you ever noticed this scenario? You're at a party and one woman seems to be commanding all the attention. It's not because she's necessarily the most beautiful or brightest or the best conversationalist, but she has something. One man approaches, sniffs, wags his tail excitedly, then suddenly, another dog (I mean man) perks up his ears, and runs over to see what's so exciting. Suddenly, before you know it, there's a pack of men circling around this one gal. Why? Because men have this hunting-dog instinct. They don't want to miss out on what the first guy has discovered. They want what he has. This is where *The Rules* went wrong when advising women to not talk to men but to just go out and circle the room with a glass of water. Glass of water? By God, give that woman some scotch—with what she's going through, not talking to a man until he talks to her. Eeeks!

No, the next time you're at a cocktail party, try this experiment—rather than isolating yourself and waiting for the illusory Mr. Right to catch your eye and approach you, talk to a nice-looking guy. Be bright and interested in this man. Be friendly. This fella will be thrilled by the attention. He'll probably think he's going to get some tonight, but the truth is, he's just your bait, because once you've started this light little conversation, you'll see the hunting dog instinct take over and before you know it, you'll be surrounded by wagging tails. I mean wagging men. Sorry, I mean very interested gentlemen.

Once you've completed your mission, walk away. Go get yourself a drink. Anything but water! And then go home—this is just the beginning of your Driving Lessons. It's a little introduction to the powers of your sex. It's been such a long time since we teased and left men wanting that we've forgotten how powerful we truly are and how much they want and need us. I'm suggesting this experiment—this flirting and then walking away without the guy, but with lots of ego strokes, instead—for two reasons. First, in the world of men, it will give you an aura of being unattainable and mysterious. The gal that got away. But more than this, not quickly getting involved with any one man will start you on the road to healing and feeling good about yourself, your desirability, your sexual powers, and will patch up some of the wounds that may have been inflicted during previous misadventures.

It's Not Your Fault

Here's the sad truth—we women tend to blame ourselves for men's brutish behavior. In fact, the world seems to blame us for being nice and trustworthy. Listen to the conservatives on talk radio. Go to your local bookstore and take note: 99 percent of the books on relationships are directed toward women, as if it's our job to fix things. As if it's our fault that relationships don't work out. As though we are the victims and we are to blame for it. Honestly, go to your local bookstore and you'll see two hundred and twenty-seven books directed toward women to make their relationships with men work and three books for men on how to get laid.

Bastards!

Okay, calm down. Let's look at the deeper meaning here. The world is telling us that men only want sex and they're not particularly interested in working on their relationships. We are also being told that if a relationship isn't working out, it's our fault. You will not see one book in Barnes & Noble on why and how men should stop being such horndogs. Why is that? Because the world applauds a horndog. He's practically an international hero. In fact, horndogs have an annual competition in Copenhagen where they compete for prizes ranging from the slightly soiled panties of starlets to huge amounts of cash and free cars.

Okay, I made that last part up.

But actually—as an aside—did you know that in Japan they have vending machines where men can buy the previously used white cotton panties supposedly worn by genuine Japanese schoolgirls? Isn't that interesting?

It must be some primal remnants from the smell of the hunt.

Deconstructing the Cad

Let's take another look at the romantic journey of our favorite cad, Rick Marin (from *Cad: Confessions of a Toxic Bachelor*). When he first meets his Ilene, she ignores him. Later, during an evening of milk and cookies, Rick asks his downstairs neighbor if she thinks Ilene is to be his future wife. To this, mommy—I mean, his friend—responds, using reverse psychology on the poor boy, "No. Too tough. You don't want to work that hard."

The next time Rick runs into Ilene it's at the Algonquin where she is surrounded by an admiring coterie of men in the publishing industry, one of them being her ex-boyfriend, Malucci, whose cigar she puffs while mercilessly teasing Rick about his horndog ways. Embarrassed, Rick makes a speedy retreat. So, what does he do next? Rick becomes Ilene's new "walker." After three months of dating, they actually go parking and neck. But no sex, not yet.

Months go by, and Rick goes through a lot. His father dies, and he grows up a bit. Finally, at the end of the summer, in the Hamptons, they consummate their love.

Did you get all that?

Well, let's deconstruct the book a little. Ask yourself, what does Ilene have that the other women swimming in what the cad refers to as New York City's "constant influx and outflux of women, the eternal chick renewal," do not have?

* She boosts his ego and helps his career.
* She is an illusive prize coveted by other men.
* She has an ex-boyfriend who is still trying to maneuver his way back into her life.
* She's intellectually challenging.
* She's not forthcoming in her affections. She makes him wait a long, long time for sex.
* She plays hot and cold. She's unpredictable.
* She cooks!
* She borrows her parents' Mercedes and the two of them drive around the neighborhood looking for this old golf guy so they can egg his house, as if they never graduated past the tenth grade. (She's fun. Oh, and her parents own a really nice car.)
* She is different. She is not Spanish, like Rick. She is Jewish, but at the end of the memoir, Rick notices that "the hem on her black lace skirt looks sort of Spanish."
* She's on to his wicked ways and won't let him get away with his caddish antics anymore.

Rick decides he will marry Ilene before he even sleeps with her. I'd like to repeat that: Rick decides he will marry Ilene before he even sleeps with her. Young Drivers, are you taking notes?

So, while it's true sex drives men, easy sex does not drive them. It's the hunt, the wait, the struggle, the torture, the building desire, and finally the consummation. Ah, it's rapture.

As loath as I am to admit it, perhaps, after all, the cads are not so different from us.

So, let the games begin.

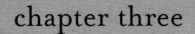

chapter three

Games Men Play

Read Machiavelli lately?
Men have.

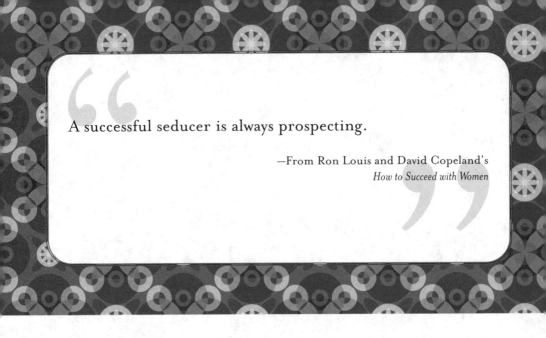

It's not that men are such bad guys. They are just very smart. They know what they want and they know how to get what they want. Most men are not evil or cruel. They love women. They love sex. They love lots of women and lots of sex. There's nothing wrong with this. It's in their nature. It's not really in their nature to go slow and then settle down with one woman. Not really. Men do not enjoy the prospect of losing their freedom, missing out on opportunities to roam the world searching for new women, different women, exotic women—hunting them down and capturing them and then moving on to new sexual adventures. For them, the idea of committing to the supposed ideal mate is a form of entropy, an end to the life force. It makes them really sad. The image of a house in Connecticut, two little kids, a yard, and a Saturday afternoon of raking leaves sends them running for the hills. To a guy, it just doesn't sound like much fun. It sounds like they're going to be kicked out of the free candy store and kept prisoner in Laura Ashley hell where they will be slowly suffocated by floral prints, bathroom cupboards overflowing with makeup and feminine hygiene products, and oh yeah, pink chintz.

And Suppose a Bunny Needs His Help?!

We've been very accommodating—giving men the keys to the candy store, thinking that one day they will get their fill and want to settle down with one woman. But the truth is, no matter how we laugh at the notion of men with their zillions of sperm waiting to let themselves loose on the world and impregnate (or symbolically impregnate) as many women as possible—there is something deep to this impulse. After all, our world is full of options and possibilities—especially the sexed-up world of today. Suppose a man does stop his philandering ways to choose one woman, and focus on one woman alone—well, then he cuts himself off from all the other beautiful babes out there. He cuts himself off from possibility, new conquests, the next big thing. And suppose this happens—the day after he commits, a Playboy Bunny sits next to him on the subway, puts her hand on his thigh, and tearfully tells him, "Oh, Hef is treating me so badly. He just ignores me and the other bunnies don't talk to me because they're jealous of my extra-big and perky—but completely natural—breasts and oh, I'm so lonely in the Playboy Mansion. I could really use some tender loving care!" Well, there's a problem. A terrible dilemma for our gentleman. How can he refuse to help out a bunny in distress?

So, why should a man focus on one woman? Why should a man commit? Why marry, for that matter? To a man, marriage is death. No, not literal death, but certainly the death of his single, free, roaming, womanizer male-self. The death of his boyhood. The death of his freedom. The death of the possibility of bedding a Playboy Bunny!

Men see marriage as a trap. This is difficult for us to quite fathom because we don't see it as a trap but rather a commitment, an agreement that we will help each other, support each other, build a life together. To us, (as deluded as this may actually be) there is a delicious sense of safety in marriage—it is the end of one-night stands or crazy guys who turn on us or the fall-out of intentionally or unintentionally breaking a heart or having our own hearts broken. To us, marriage means committed love, a home together, perhaps children and eventually, growing old and walking into the sunset, holding hands and discussing how the past fifty years of togetherness have been so very splendid.

This scenario makes men want to scream at the top of their lungs and then shoot themselves in the head and have the whole bloody thing done with.

This is because they don't see marriage as such a great deal. While our society is still (unfortunately) an unfair and more dangerous place for women than for men and it may be in a woman's interest to have one partner, this is not the case for men. Also, while both men and women might want children, women's fertility is limited. According to the article "Party Now, Pay Later?" in the September 2004 issue of *Elle*, from age thirty to thirty-four, one in every seven couples experience infertility, and at forty to forty-four, it jumps to one in four. In the meantime, most men can have children into their dotage. Many of them do. It's certainly not unusual to see a forty-something-year-old guy who's spent a good twenty years building his career, making money, and playing the field finally marry and start a family with a twenty-eight-year-old.

We are still living in an age where women are earning seventy-five cents for every dollar that men earn. Therefore, it is not such a bad idea for us to combine our resources with a man's. For a man, marriage may cost a great deal. He is giving up a kind of sexual freedom that our society supports and applauds rather than frowns upon. He has the additional burden of financial obligations should his spouse happen to be less than a brilliant breadwinner, and should there be children. And with children come complications and the big male fear—that his wife will pay more attention to the helpless crying baby in the crib in the next room and ignore her sexually voracious husband who has been patiently waiting a good twenty minutes in the bed after a hard day's work for his well-deserved blow job!

Men, Women, Sex, and Status

So, think about it—with all these disadvantages—why would men marry?

Well, of course the answer we would like to hear is "because they've fallen in love!" But, I suspect, men marry for much more pragmatic reasons. Without the desperate, unfulfilled need for sex clouding his judgment, today's man tends to marry for very strategic, well-thought-out reasons. He chooses a woman who will add to his status in the world, especially in the world of other men. Men gain status from their association with different sorts of women, depending on their profession and their position in their community. Some get great kudos for the very young and beautiful trophy wife ("Hey, how did Bob snag that Victoria's Secret model?" "Well, I hear he's hung like a horse!"). Others gain a leg up by marrying women who are wealthy ("Wow, did you see that yacht she bought him?" "Yeah, well, you know he's hung like a horse."). Or they may align themselves with the boss's daughter or a gal who will help their career ("Bob is marrying the prime minister of India?" "Yeah well, you know about his…").

Okay, I am being facetious here. But men do look at another man's girlfriend or wife as a reflection of how well he is doing in the world. The right woman can add the same kind of status to a man as owning an expensive car or big house. And on the other hand, the wrong woman can cause a fella's standing in the world to plummet.

Analyzing Love, Actually

Contrary to what popular literature and film tell us, men like to marry up rather than down. A few years ago the film Love, Actually revealed how Hollywood is still spoon-feeding its female viewers the Pretty Woman/Cinderella myth. Each of the men in this film suffers deeply from the effects of love. These men see love as the worst thing that could possibly happen to them. In fact, Hugh Grant's character supposedly suffers so much that he is often tongue-tied and paralyzed. They are in love with their maid, their assistant, their secretary, their best friend's wife, but it takes these fumbling men an excruciatingly long time to act upon this "love," despite the fact that the female objects of desire are below them—status-wise. Only one male in the movie truly aspires to capture the heart of a female who is in an elevated position. She is a beautiful singer, the star of a show. She is seemingly unattainable. She is popular and well-loved. She is poised and she is about to leave the country. What does our hero do? First, he takes up the drums (having never studied music in his life), so that he can be a musical accompaniment in her show. Next he chases her to the airport, breaks through security, sprints through all sorts of gates and guards, screams her name through the glass in homage to the wedding scene in *The Graduate* and finally, finally catches up with his heroine.

Here's the startling part about this fella. Unlike his male counterparts in *Love, Actually*, he is not a grownup. He is nine years old. And he's the only virgin in the movie.

What are we to make of this? Perhaps that only a virgin boy-child would go to such extraordinary lengths to woo a woman. Or perhaps that grown men, distracted by their plethora of sexual possibilities, have become paralyzed by choice. And is the darker message, directed to the male viewer, that when they do make a choice, they are making one that lowers their status in the world rather than elevates it? Is the subtext of the film, subliminally directed at the male audience, that to commit is to lose status? So, while women are weeping in the audience, imagining that like the coffee-serving Cinderella secretary they, too, will be chosen by the Prince Charming prime minister, the male viewer takes in this story as a cautionary tale on the pitfalls of romantic love and thinks, "Oh my god, what an awful fate it is for the prime minister of England to end up with this potty-mouthed gal and her bourgeois family from the dodgy part of town." And in particular, American male viewers are probably thinking, "Gee, that chubby dark-haired assistant girl with the potty mouth looks a lot like Monica Lewinsky. Why doesn't he just do what our president did?"

Well, of course he's not going to do what our president did, because we've learned our lesson. Our national psyche has been made to pay an enormous price for President Clinton's brush with *flagrante delicto*. We as a nation have been chastised and chastened—and so we've entered an era of no more fun. Yes, we've been devastated by the attacks on the World Trade Center, but fun was already gone long before 9/11. Look at our political leaders—no matter how different each side may be when it comes to policy, they are all basically voicing the message, "I'm not like him. I'm not a horndog! I love my kids and my wife, honest!"

The Cinderella/Pretty Woman Myth

But despite all this, *Love, Actually* doesn't completely believe in itself. The final scene with the prime minister and his over-enthusiastic, red-coated, beret-wearing assistant is embarrassing. The prime minister certainly looks embarrassed, and we as Americans actually do feel a little sorry for poor little old Great Britain, paying for the sins of our president by marrying Monica Lewinsky and saving her from her Cinderella life, slaving away on her knees.

Truth be told, in today's world, prime ministers do not marry their assistants. Big businessmen who look like Richard Gere do not marry their prostitutes. And your everyday guy is not looking to marry the art school graduate with the truckload of student loan debt. I am sorry to sound so harsh, but this is the truth.

This is because once a man has his basic needs of sex, food, and shelter met, he wakes up clear-headed or at least seemingly clear-headed and highly rational. Gone are the days when men were so driven by lust that they were willing to do anything to obtain their object of desire. Men have grown plump and flaccid on an endless feeding of available sex.

It's a very simple equation—if men are driven by their need for sex and we constantly give them an all-you-can-eat buffet of sex, well then there's no need to work, struggle, and strive for sex. So, what do men do with their energies? Well they put that drive into making more money, inventing more widgets, stocking our stores with more unnecessary products, and oh yeah, starting wars.

It goes like this—in the light of morning after a good night of schtuping, or better yet, some excellent fellatio where the guy can simply lie back and relax, he wants to check his Excel spreadsheets. Or watch a baseball game or buy some stocks or count the decimal points in his bank accounts. He wants to do anything with numbers. This is because men fear that loss of bodily fluids after sex, so they want to compensate for losing a thousand sperm by adding thousands to their checking account. It makes them feel full again. It gets them excited about life and all its possibility. This is because men know that in order to attract women they need resources. Some more than others.

Why Steve Martin Is a Genius

In Steve Martin's delicious novella, *Shop Girl*, our Prince Charming, the wealthy Mr. Ray Porter, does not marry the Cinderella Shop Girl. This is a brilliant, smart, and deeply moving literary choice on Mr. Martin's part, because the reality is that in today's world, no one really believes the millionaire gentleman would actually marry and rescue the poor shop girl, twenty years his junior, who's fallen deeply and madly in love with him. Sad, in a way, isn't it? He is in love with her too, but no, he is not going to marry her. So, it's sad for him. Sad for her. Sad for us. Ultimately, she gets her heart broken by Mr. Ray Porter, and by another man, until finally she reunites with a boy her own age who sells souped-up amplifiers. One wonders, is the message of the book stick to your own kind? Don't try to marry up? Is this part of the new chastising—a more realistic story with an anti-*Pretty Woman* conclusion? Are we being told, you can have an affair with a man of higher status and he will give you money for your Prozac prescription and even pay off your student-loan debt, but don't expect him to commit to you? By the book's end, our older, wiser millionaire, Mr. Ray Porter, tells us he has "become her parent, and she his child," and our shop girl has this realization: "She has learned that her body is precious and it mustn't be offered carelessly ever again, as it holds a direct connection to her heart."

This is from Steve Martin—a savvy, funny, urbane, sophisticated, and talented writer and actor. What is going on here?

As women, we are being given full disclosure. We are being clearly warned that men are not particularly motivated to commit.

Friends with Benefits

Men are much more rational than we are when it comes to relationships. In fact, many men, after being completely satisfied, will look at you, lying peacefully asleep in the bed next to them, and think, "I wonder what other benefits I could derive from this arrangement?" Don't laugh! You'd be surprised how men have an uncanny ability to parlay a sexual liaison into something more. The truth is, some men do not simply want sex. They want sex and:

1. A free place to stay in NYC for a month until they can move to Montana.
2. To make his ex-girlfriend really, really jealous.

3. To option your screenplay and make a lot of money off you.

4. To borrow your car.

5. To get you to introduce them to your hot cousin (oooh, and maybe have a threesome!).

6. Maid service.

7. Some free home-cookin'!

8. To hang out with your cool ex-brother-in-law who has season tickets to the Bears games.

9. To borrow money from you.

10. To shack up with you while his wife comes back to her senses and takes him in again.

11. Oh yeah, and to have sex with you too, if that's cool.

The point is, once sexually satisfied, men become very clear-headed about their relationship with their lover and they see no need to rescue the poor shop girl/Cinderella/assistant/maid/waif/art school grad with student loans. I sincerely apologize if I am destroying all your heartfelt beliefs and dreams, but think of it this way: get to work, make some money, pull yourself up by your bootstraps, and make something of yourself. You'll be happier that way and you'll attract many, many suitors, because you will have status. Yes, when you have status (and money), you will have many more men interested in you and you will have many men vying for your attention—because as you've learned by now, men thrive on competition. Once you've got this kind of status, you can pick and choose and be very fussy about whom you want to be with.

Shop Girls of the World Unite!

I know, I know. If you're really struggling financially and have few professional prospects, it's really hard to elevate your status. In my more paranoid, conspiracy-theory moments, I believe the financial and professional inequities we women suffer through are all part of men's nefarious plan to keep poor shop girls trapped in a place where we must gratefully accept the position of sexual servitude— whether it's the mistress whose rent is paid for, or the secretary who gets extra bonuses for "overtime," or the girl who feels forced to sleep with her date in order to have an expensive meal and go to a Broadway show every now and then, because she just can't afford to do these things herself. You see, it is in men's sexual interest to keep us from earning as much as they do. It means, women need them, and women are grateful.

The Economics of Sex

Men, through their Machiavellian machinations, have put women at an economic disadvantage by downgrading our value and flooding the market with identical silicone-implanted blonde babes who look startlingly like Pamela Anderson wannabes and offer sex-sex-sex twenty-four hours a day in thirty-six different varieties and twenty-seven new flavors. It's as simple as the law of supply and demand:

1. Flood the marketplace.
2. Undervalue the product.
3. Slash prices.
4. Yippee, free sex for all!

Only thing is, you never had to pay for it, did you? So where is the bargain for women? Well, there is none. We've just been hoodwinked once again. It's true, we want the attention, we want the male gaze. We want them to hunger for us, pursue us, work to get us, suffer a little—all in the name of passion and rapture. We want love. True and abiding love.

But do not despair, because there is hope. We can fight back.

Let's raise the value of our own sex. Let's take it back. Now, this doesn't mean you're going to wear a sack and a headscarf and an iron maiden, but how about rediscovering the allure of the mysterious. How about a little intrigue? How about going slow?

Think of the iconic librarian with the hair in the bun, the white pearls, the eyeglasses, the skirt that seems modest enough, but hugs her derriere in a most provocative way.

Think of driving to Vermont and first encountering a mountain. First, it is shrouded in fog. Around every curve of the road, it slowly reveals itself, coming in and out of view, one side exposed, then hidden. The other side exposed, then disappears from view. Even nature knows how to be coy.

Return to Rapture

There's a wonderful organization called Slow Food. It was founded in 1986 with a mission to protect the pleasures of the table from the homogenization of fast food and modern life. It promotes gastronomic culture, develops taste education, conserves agricultural biodiversity, and protects traditional foods at risk of extinction. Wow.

So here's what I'm suggesting. Let's protect the pleasure of sex. Let's stop the tide of homogeneous sex, fast-food sex. Let's develop some taste before real honest-to-goodness female sexuality becomes extinct.

Nothing less than our sex is at stake here because if we allow ourselves to be reduced to globes of jiggling flesh, then our individuality is lost, the culture of being female is diminished, and our very sex is just another brand of soda pop. I believe the narrator of Steve Martin's book is on to something true and fine when he tells us that the heroine "has learned that her body is precious and it mustn't be offered carelessly ever again, as it holds a direct connection to her heart."

So, let's create Slow Sex. Let's get men to appreciate us, focus on us, and take their time. Let's make men behave.

They will start off by being annoyed with the idea that they have to actually chop and peel some vegetables—I mean actually take time and listen to a woman and get to know her; her taste, texture, varieties, and style. But, if we work together, we can do it, because, after all—our body does have a direct connection to our heart.

PART TWO

A Practical Guide to Modern Romance

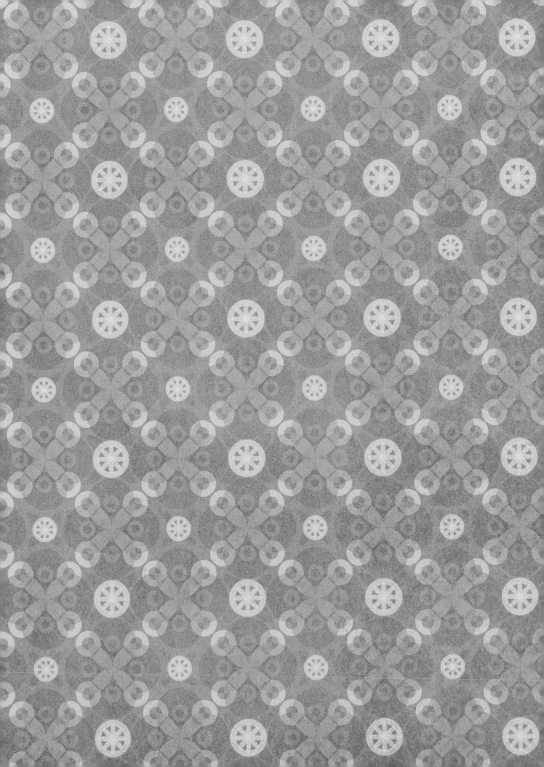

chapter four

The Art of Flirting

How to love like a Marxist

> In flirtation you never know whether the beginning of the story—the story of the relationship—will be the end; flirtation, that is to say, exploits the idea of surprise …Flirtation, if it can be sustained, is a way of cultivating wishes, playing for time.

—from *On Flirtation* by Adam Phillips

By now, you are convinced. Men want sex, but you want more than sex. But men—they mostly want sex. They are thinking about it all the time. They are thinking about it in the morning when they're brushing their teeth. They're thinking about it in line at the ATM. They're thinking about it when they're stuck in traffic on the 405. And even at the animal hospital with their aging pooch—when the hot lady vet says, "I'm so sorry, Mr. Jones, but we're going to have to put old Spikey down"—they're not thinking about all the great times they had with Spikey at the dog park. No, they're thinking about sex!

This is actually good news because it means if you want to attract a fella, you really don't have to do much work. All you really have to do is show up and look good.

All right, perhaps it's a little more complicated than that. Men do need a little encouragement. This is because they really are thinking about sex all the time, and this makes them a little nervous and they feel a little guilty about it. They don't want you to know the awful truth, so some men may actually be a bit shy and embarrassed. Light flirting can help them relax and also let them know that while you find them interesting, you have no idea what sort of horndog thoughts are going on in their sexually obsessed brain…but of course you do.

What Is Flirting?

Before we get to specific techniques, let's be clear about what flirting actually is, because there are definitely some blurry lines when it comes to this ancient art of attracting the opposite sex. First of all, flirting is not serious. It is not even sexual. It can be a little romantic, but basically, it's inconsequential. It is playful. It means to act amorously without serious intent. True, it's a tease, but it's also an excellent way for a woman to buy some time. Unfortunately, many of us have lost our gift for subtlety when it comes to flirting, and so today's man will look at a woman's derriere and say, "You want some fries with that shake?" and we consider this flirting. And you know what? That is not flirting. That's called being an idiot.

Really good, artful flirting should be as fleeting and as light as a butterfly. As long as your flirtations have no gravitas to them, no obvious hidden agendas or promises, it is not deceptive or mean. It's an important part of the courtship process. A little flirting provides you with a way to suss out whether a man is receptive to you, attracted to you, and whether he might become a potential lover. Flirting is a powerful tool, particularly for women, because it's our way of getting to know a man before there is anything at stake. It gives us a chance to get a feel for a man before our hearts and bodies are engaged. Men may know whether or not they're attracted to a woman just by her looks, but we need to be able to use our intuitive powers to decide whether a man is a worthy candidate for our affections. This may take some time, because as we know, men play games. One of the games is "let me sweep you off your feet before you can find out I have a girlfriend in Boston and another one in L.A. and I really don't work for Amtrak, I just like to hang out in train stations and do crossword puzzles and steal gum from the news stand, because basically I am a sociopath."

No, we need flirtations—the butterfly variety—so we can figure out just who this man is. Is he witty, interesting? Does he seem to have friends? A job?

Is he a nice guy? Is he safe? Sane? Is he truly available? This takes time. And if a man thinks you want him, you really want him—you know, in that carnal sense—well then, he will lie, steal, and cheat to close the deal. So don't let him know you want him or even think of him amorously for a long time. Also, this period of flirtation gives you the time to determine whether he would make a good male friend. And in order to drive men crazy, you will need lots of male friends to add to your coterie. I'll discuss what a coterie is and how to build a coterie in chapter 6.

But at the beginning of a relationship, we need a lot of information. That's why we need to flirt a lot, over a long period of time, and this is why our flirtation should be mostly light, without sexual innuendo. Flirting lays the basis for many, many things in a relationship. And this flirting must be nonsexual. We live in a dangerous world, and we must be careful that men don't get the wrong idea. So, flirting should be subtle. It's an art form that can be developed over time.

A How-To Course in the Art of Flirting

So, to begin the lessons—the first step is to try to look your best whenever you leave your home. Once out, flirt with everyone. Light flirting, whether it's with the young guy at the deli or the elderly lady selling books or the married professor from New Haven can be fun, great practice, and a terrific confidence-builder. No, you're not going to sleep with the young guy, the elderly lady, or the married professor. You are just having fun and enjoying humanity. You are making friends. You are building a reputation for being a friendly person. You see, flirting is good for the planet! It makes our lives more interesting and lively. Flirting does not have to be made up of incredibly witty banter. In fact, at the start it should be quite simple and straightforward. All you need to do is encourage conversation, a little exchange. How? Like this:

* Comment on the obvious. "Oh my God! It's pouring rain out there!"
* Ask for assistance. "Do you know where I can buy an umbrella?"
* Compliment. "Wow, you really know about umbrella stores!"

Men Love Compliments (Don't We All?)

Do not underestimate this last flirtation, especially when it comes to men. Men are absolute suckers for compliments, praise, and appreciation. Just read John Gray's *Men Are from Mars, Women Are from Venus*. Here's what he says men need: trust, acceptance, appreciation, admiration, approval, encouragement. That basically translates into, "Thank you so much for telling me about the umbrella store. I really appreciate it. Wow, I really admire the fact you know so much about where to buy an umbrella. I encourage you to tell more people about umbrella stores!" And you could add, "I think you're so smart, you could open up your own umbrella store!" but only if it sounds encouraging and not as if you're trying to improve his lot in life. According to John Gray, you should never try to improve men because they find this very upsetting and smothering and it reminds them of their mother—okay, he didn't exactly say the part about being like their mother, but you get the drift. At any rate, if you don't like the fact that he does nothing all day but hang out and direct people to the nearest umbrella store, don't say anything about it. He knows what he's doing and you should just mind your own business.

But seriously, why should you concern yourself with the fact that he hangs out in the rain all day talking with whomever passes by—you are just flirting.

And you are developing your art. You'll find that these quick, inconsequential conversations will build your confidence. This confidence-building is essential at the beginning of your training, so keep things light and quick. Even if you're very attracted to a man and believe there is a true rapport, you should still leave the exchange quickly before he has a chance to figure out whether you are really attracted to him or not. At this stage, he should always be kept wondering. This is not a game; this is simply being smart and not putting all your eggs in one basket. Men are certainly not putting all their eggs in one basket. In fact, the fellas who wrote *How to Succeed with Women* advise men to flirt with many women all the time so that they can have dozens of women to call in an instant and sleep with that night. That night. On call, so to speak. Men pursue lots and lots of women—because they know there's going to be that lonely, desperate evening when they'll need a quick fix. You don't want to be a guy's fix. So be friendly and fun and get the hell out.

Be an Equal-Opportunity Flirt

When you get into conversations with lots of different people—the old man waiting on you at the deli, the guy at the drycleaner's, the clerk at the post office—you'll discover that people are thrilled to talk about themselves. When you ask a guy about something he's an expert at—say, how to get spots out of linen—you'll find that people truly light up. You'll learn all sorts of new things about people and their professions and interests. You'll make everyone's day a little brighter and you'll become more comfortable with men and you'll build up your sexual chi.

Yes, your sexual chi. It's like this, you have a certain amount of sexual chi—the power to attract, a kind of sensual energy. If you hold on to it and only release this chi, this sexual power, when you are with a man who really, really excites you—a viable candidate—and if you seldom flirt, then when you do, you'll feel awkward because there is too much at stake. You're bound to feel anxious. There's the possibility that you will fall into bed with a man much too quickly and much less artfully than you would like, especially if he's the only guy you flirt with.

On the other hand, if you are constantly giving away your sexual chi and actually consummating every other flirtation that comes your way, then you will find yourself feeling depleted at some point—especially if the gentlemen in question are of the "catch and release" variety.

So, how does one build up sexual chi and keep it flowing? Flirt with everyone. Enjoy life, but do not give yourself completely away. Practice the art of nonattachment. As you cultivate the art of flirtation, you will forget that you are actually flirting, but you will begin to feel a greater sense of possibility.

Also, if you become known as a gal who is just very friendly, then a man cannot assume that your quick banter, your light flirtations, are any cause for him to presume that you are insanely attracted to him and that he might add you to his basket of eggs. This is important, because you want to keep men guessing. A man unsure of his place in your heart is more likely to focus his attention on you, because he's captivated by the thrill of the hunt, the one that got away.

The Butterfly Effect

You'll find that after a few weeks of this equal-opportunity flirting, your sense of your own desirability will soar. Men will flirt back with you, because, yes, men are always trawling for sex, but as long as you are not promising anything—either by word or action—you are not teasing or misleading. You are just being friendly. The authors of *What Men Want* tell us all we have to do is look at a guy, smile, stand near him, and say hello. They say, "The only way a woman can make the wrong impression is by outright sexual innuendo," because if you do, a guy is going to get the wrong impression.

When you keep your conversation light, free of double entendres, a man can't assume or even suggest that you go back to his apartment with him. (And please—when men ask you back to their apartment—this isn't a compliment.

If they think they're going to get some, they'll ask anyone who's breathing! So no, being invited up to their pad for a quickie is not a compliment!) So keep your flirtations innocent. The man must know for certain that it is just a flirtation, not a promise, not a proposal. This is especially true if you have a boyfriend or husband already. You certainly don't want to get into hot water. In fact, if you're already involved with a fella, he should be aware of your flirtations, but also assured that they are not serious and not a threat to your relationship. And suppose you are flirting with one fella, but actually want to ignite the passions of another—well then, the flirtation must still be very subtle. This way, the true object of your affections is kept alert by the sense of competition, but he will not get the impression that you are actually giving your heart to someone else.

Therefore, it's important to vigilantly keep your flirtations light. This means you talk about general things. Flatter, but don't get too personal. Be imaginative.

You can see the difference between these two styles. Good flirting means showing an interest, but not inserting a subtle or not-so-subtle sexual agenda into the conversation. Successful flirting means entering into their world.

Good Flirtation Line	*Bad Flirtation Line*
I really like your suit. Is it Armani?	I really like your suit. Armani makes me hot!
Do you know where the next plenary session is being held?	Can I sit next to you at the next plenary session?
I really enjoyed your lecture.	Your lecture made me hot.
What did you mean when you said there's a new system for uranium/ thorium dating?	I loved it whenever you said uranium. Hmmmm.
You have a dangerous mind.	You have a dangerous body.

Let them know you've actually been listening and paying attention. You are not just interested in bedding a man; you want to first get to know how his mind works. If you are complimentary—especially about his work rather than his personal appearance—the man in question will be left with good feelings about you, because you've asked him about himself. You've flattered the man and this makes him feel great. Men have a Pavlovian response to flattery and as they begin to associate you with happy thoughts, they will return again and again.

But You're Only Interested in His Mind

Do not find yourself alone with a man, but rather arrange to have witnesses to your light flirtations. Men want what other men have—the hound dogs—so why not give them something to chew on? But again, keep things from getting too provocative. Men will push you into erotic situations by spicing their conversation with double entendres and dirty jokes. They'll try to get you inebriated and isolated. "Oh, let's go visit the empty ballroom on the seventeenth floor." They'll come up with any excuse to touch you. "That necklace is lovely. Can I touch it?" Their compliments will center on physicality—your mouth, your lips, your breasts, your bottom. Before you know it, you're making out with a stranger in an empty ballroom on the seventeenth floor and you can't remember what happened to the silver necklace your mother gave you on your twenty-first birthday!

The Morning After

Of course it is intoxicating—that high we get from male attention, the compliments, the focus, the unmistakable feeling that he's after something and that something is you. But that's why you should avoid it. It's not real. It's a kind of drug that courses through our body and then is gone the next morning. For a man, too, this kind of quick seduction is addictive. Once he obtains his high from conquering one woman, he wants another woman and another and another. That's his addiction. Yes, his addiction. This is because men get a lot out of sex. More than just sex. Some men use sex as a drug to help them escape from the workaday world. Some use it because conquering and bedding a woman gives them extra vim and vigor and makes them feel powerful and strong, just like eating a big bowl of Wheaties. Some just want to relax and for them, sex is a tranquilizer, a salve for their world-weariness. For some, it's a great ego boost, something they can brag about to their friends later. The point is, you don't want to become anyone's drug of choice because no matter how exciting the high is for you as well as for him, he will resent his own neediness and he will resent you. And you will certainly begin to resent him.

Get the Attention You Deserve

But consider what flirtation without consummation gets you—attention. A lot of attention. Focus. Interested men. Lots of them. And as women, we thrive on attention. Flirtation with delayed consummation builds our ego and makes us feel great. It's like sunshine and we blossom under the warmth of the male gaze. So flirt, but remember it's just window-shopping. Nothing is bought or sold.

So, here's what you need to flirt:

* Look good.
* Be interested (especially in his work), but not intense.
* Compliment, praise, approve, appreciate.
* Smile, but no sexual innuendos allowed.
* Keep it light.
* Exit quickly.

One note on "looking good." This means looking nice, but not so provocative that no matter what you say, no matter how light your conversation is, your clothing is saying, "Fuck me now!" So, if you dress and move like Britney Spears—well, actually, if you dress like Britney Spears then you need to stop it immediately.

Test His Intelligence

Now, if you're not comfortable with flattering and praising a man, there are other ways to flirt that are still subtle and enticing. You might challenge him— "Do you really believe that a UFO landed in Utah in 1957? That seems impossible to me!" However, this only works if he happens to be an UFO expert and is just waiting for a gal to challenge his authority. It's a reverse form of praise. Basically, you simply find the man's area of knowledge and confidence and you give him an excuse to expound a little. Men love to expound.

Be a Good Listener

Your flirting style is your own, but it's important to get to know the man in question —where does he feel most confident, most insecure? What are his fondest childhood memories? His secret dreams and ambitions? All this information will help you to hone your art. So listen carefully at the beginning. And when in doubt, smile and ask questions. That can be very powerful all by itself.

Okay, the next step to successful flirtation is to turn some of the fellas into your friends. Yes, friends. Not lovers. Just friends. Men hate this. It really drives them crazy. But, it's very good for you. So, look for candidates—and begin forming a group of men with whom you are not intimate, but under the right circumstances, you might be. Start today by cultivating male friends who flirt with you, but can be effectively held at arm's length.

Look Like You're Having Fun

And get busy with your life. You may think that men will ignore you if you're very involved with your work, your friends, your family, your passions, but the truth is this sparks men's interest in you. They wonder what's going on with you when you're not around and they fear that perhaps another fella is going to get to you before them. When we're dressed up, going out, happy, busy with our own lives, it puts men on their best behavior. It's the sales-rack phenomenon. Have you ever walked into a store and found a rack of great summer frocks on sale? No one is around and you feel like you've discovered gold. You quietly go through the dresses, gently pulling out the ones you want to try on in the fitting room, when suddenly you're surrounded by a pack of gals who have picked up the scent of the sale—and now they're all around you, looking for the perfect dress.

Well, it's like that with men. Men are lazy and uninterested when they think they've got you figured out, when they know where you are and when you're there and that you're just waiting around for their phone call. They get bored when they think they know you and that there's nothing you can do to surprise them. But, begin to think about straying, just think about it, and suddenly, they're back at your doorstep with a bouquet of roses.

Penises Have Ears

I apologize for this expression, but it's true—penises have ears. Yes. Here's an example of how this works: You've been dating a fella for a quite awhile. You've been having great sex and things are going splendidly. One night, you're on the phone and he seems particularly cranky. Somehow you get into an argument about *The Naked and the Dead* and he says, "Yeah, well I disagree! I think

Norman Mailer is a genius!" But before you can say anything else, he says, "Oh, hold on. I've got another call." Click. And that's it. Yes, that's it. He never calls back. You wait by the phone for an hour. He doesn't call back. He doesn't call back the next day or the day after that. You call him, but get his machine and you say, "Are you okay? You said you were going to call me back." And still, weeks go by and he doesn't call back. You imagine maybe he's really, really sensitive about Norman Mailer and you really upset him. You call and leave a message saying, "Listen, I'm rereading Mailer right now and I think maybe you're right. Anyway, I'm sorry about what I said." More weeks go by. Months go by and he doesn't call back. You get on with your life. You buy a new couch. Your cat dies. You get a big promotion. You're transferred to London. You are getting over the Norman Mailer guy. You hardly ever think of him anymore. Then one day in January, you meet this wonderful man named Frederick. He's British and cute and he works for the government. One night, it's snowing outside and you are getting cuddly with Fred. In fact, you are about to artfully succumb to Fred's charms. And at this very inopportune moment—guess who calls you? The Norman Mailer guy! Yes, he's back! He misses you. But why is he calling now, after all this time? Well, ladies, it's because penises have ears.

Be Dangerous

So, how can you use this knowledge to help you get what you want? Give him something to keep him alert. This is especially necessary once you're in a committed relationship or married. Married men have a tendency to turn their wives into security blankets, encouraging evenings at home and the safety of routine. Don't fall for this—it's a ruse! Once a man feels he "has" you and there is a strong sense of attachment, he will grow antsy and want to rebel. Yes, just like a little boy who wants to get away from his mommy. Don't ever let him see you as his mommy or a safety blanket or predictable or safe. Be dangerous. Unpredictable. And definitely get the hell out of the house!

This is why a lifetime of flirting and building your group of admirers will add to your mystique. These men are not lovers, just friends. But they like you, and their very existence will keep all the men in your life focused, vying for your attention. This is because men need to be constantly reminded that if they are not careful, they can always be replaced.

How They Do It in Hollywood

So how do you keep the various males in your life circling around, but not too close to be bothersome? You "buff" them. I'm borrowing this expression from Hollywood producers, who hang out in nice offices all day, reading *Variety*, drinking chai lattes, and hoping that one of these days the studio will actually greenlight one of their projects. They have a thing called "buffing." Buffing basically means keeping up with contacts through phone or email. It means sending a note or a book or a letter of congratulations.

You can do this too. Simply remind your buffees of your existence so that they begin to associate your name with pleasant thoughts. Just call them up every now and then, send a note, meet for lunch. It's nothing serious—it's absolutely not sexual—but it's enough so that they won't forget you. You will need this group more than ever once you become married or become involved with one man.

A Gal Needs a Cover

It's helpful to use the guise of work or hobbies or some other interest to form flirtations. A gal needs a kind of "cover" so that the man is never quite sure of her true intentions. This uncertainty gives us a lot of leverage and buys much-needed time. Our flirtations and the men we "buff" should all come out of the natural course of our day, our life, our work. It's better for a man to think that we're terribly career-minded or ambitious or passionate about chess than to think we are hungry and desirous of him. So, create a cover. Passion will reveal itself, but let things simmer and come to a slow boil. After all, love takes time.

If you're on a date and there is one man sitting across from you, he knows you must be somewhat interested in him—otherwise you wouldn't be there. So, how do you slow him down when it's clear there's more at stake than a simple friendship? This gets tricky, especially if you're using a dating service, because the man comes to the date already knowing you're in the market for romance. Even in this situation, however, you can leave him feeling a little off-kilter. Defuse the conversation immediately by talking about light things. Don't reveal your entire history. Remain a mystery. Don't divulge every detail of your life. This is good advice for many reasons. First of all, you want to intrigue him, but more than this, you need to get to know him better. The first thing you must do in this initial meeting is to immediately "close your purse" and tell him you are really only window-shopping. You don't really need a new car—I mean, a new man. You are just thinking about it. But don't tell him this literally. Rather, show him this through gesture and lack of intense conversation. Be cool.

And suppose you are mad for him and want to hop into the sack immediately. Suppose, my God, you've waited long enough and you're dying to have sex and he's so cute and why should you play these stupid games? You want sex!!!!

Save Your Calories

Control yourself. Get hold of your impulses. We do this with food and exercise, don't we? Okay, so we can do it with sex. Don't waste your calories on cads. Trust me, it'll pay off in the end. So flirt. Like a butterfly.

Men will want to move from the arena of flirtations to something more substantial very quickly. This is because they are always prospecting, always looking for potential sex wherever they go, and when they see what looks like a sure thing, they will want to close the deal as quickly and efficiently as possible. Therefore, you must do everything you can to keep the man at bay—so that the flirtation takes a long, long time. As long as possible. This way, you can put him on probation. You can find out what he's like before you let him into your bedroom. This is the time when you have all the power—during the flirtation stage when he is at complete attention—starved for your touch, wriggling on your hook, willing to do anything to please you. Yes! Keep him right there for a good long time.

How do you do that—how do you entice a man through flirtation that's obvious enough to keep him hooked, but light enough that he'll remain at bay and not become a jerk and attack or accuse you of being a cocktease?

Just as an aside—isn't it interesting how you hardly ever hear that word anymore? Is that because we've been completely cowed into never, ever teasing another cock again? Is this because cocks are so dangerous and powerful and sensitive that they might suddenly explode and create a nuclear war? Is this why we sleep with men whom perhaps we really just wanted to court and spark? Have we actually been pushed into sexual liaisons because it was easier to comply than to cry rape and raise a ruckus? Is this moratorium on nonsexual flirtation just another way men have kept us in line? And what about the cocks—do you ever wonder if they miss being teased? And is it really such a horribly dangerous thing—a teased cock?

The Body/Heart Connection

So, what's a gal to do? Well, first of all, you cannot be accused of being a tease if you are not overtly sexual and you have some very good reasons for not sleeping with the man in question. You are not "playing hard to get." You are simply hard to get. And why shouldn't we be hard to get? Men are hard to get when it comes to commitment—and so we're hard to get when it comes to sex. Isn't that fair? The authors of *What Men Want* tell us that a man will oftentimes not call a woman, even though he said he would, because it's "a defense mechanism men use to keep their vulnerability at a minimum." So, why shouldn't we too, have a defense mechanism? Don't we deserve to protect our vulnerabilities? But here's the amazing thing about our being hard to get (not simply playing at it): men are inspired by it, especially if it is presented in an authentic way. If you can get to know a man, become friends, and encourage him through flattery, interest, kindness, and appreciation, he will wait a long time to have sex with you. When we do this, we are not game players (like many men out there), we're just taking care of ourselves. We're not letting some bloke toy with our feelings, because yes, our bodies are connected to our hearts. And men better get used to it and straighten up!

This may seem like a time-waster to you. You may wonder, "When do I stop accumulating male friends and get myself the perfect boyfriend, regular sex, that trip to Aruba, and a date for Valentine's Day? Come on, I'm in a hurry!" We tend to think this way because we are living in such a capitalist country and so it's difficult to reimagine the nature of love. We've been trained to think of love as an acquisition. We think of dating as something we order from a catalog. I'll get that in pink, size medium, without the side stitching. Oh, and send that rush delivery!

What I am suggesting here is more than simply slowing down the dating process, but bringing Zen into the art of romance. Forget about getting there (wherever "there" is—sex or marriage or whatever). How about being in the moment? How about flirting for the sake of flirting? How about exploring the nature of love and romance without any goal in mind? Forget about those rules—the yin: "never accept a date for Saturday night if he doesn't call by Wednesday" and the yang: "You must have sex after the third date."

Love Is Not a Latté

Flirt, because it's fun and delightful and makes the world a more pleasant place to be in. We must retrain our men to know that when we flirt, it does not necessarily mean they're going to get laid. Flirting introduces a kind of chaos into the orderly world of men because it is not a transaction. It does not make sense. Any more than a butterfly makes sense. Our corporate go-getters will try to sell flirtation, romance. They will try to brand it and turn it into the Starbucks of sex. This is what dating services, speed-dating, match-making, and Internet pornography are all about—turning love and sex into a commodity and then making that commodity easy to sell, buy, and dispose of when we're done. But love will never be orderly and therefore it can never be an easy transaction. It's dangerous stuff. It involves the heart. It brings irrationality into this orderly world of buying and selling. When it comes to flirting, there is no *quid pro quo*. There is no such thing as getting what you paid for. It is never even-steven. There is no exchange. It is topsy-turvy. Unpredictable. Deeply meaningful and meaning absolutely nothing. Flirting is always flirting with disaster. That's what makes it so thrilling, so dangerous, so enticing, and in a world where so many men are on the prowl—stealthy cat burglars of the heart—flirtation is a gal's best defense.

chapter five

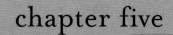

Where the Boys Are

They're all around you

> **Men are like buses. If you miss one, there's always another one coming around the corner.**
>
> —Author unknown

They're all over the place! Open your window and look out. There's the mailman and the UPS guy. There's your neighbor, your coworker, your teacher, the guy at the supermarket, the man selling newspapers. There's your cousin, your best friend's brother, your sister's chiropractor, your doctor's nephew, the man who sat next to you at jury duty, the fella from the graphic design firm, and the man standing three feet away from you in the bookstore.

Okay, most of these men are wrong for you. Inappropriate. Maybe not even attractive. So, what do you do? Well, you don't ignore them and walk away with your nose in the air. No. You practice on them, talk to them. Begin a light, inconsequential conversation. Go ahead and enjoy a man's company for nothing more than the delight of meeting someone new and having a nice conversation. You are not promising anything. You are not committing to anything. But you'll find that nine out of ten times a little conversation or comment will perk up a man's interest and he will focus a little more on you—wondering if you want something more—perhaps a drink, dinner, a quick roll in the hay. Men can't help having thoughts like this. But of course you don't want any of those things. You are simply letting his attention fill your sails. This is good chi, baby.

Maybe the UPS man isn't the guy you want to have a mad passionate affair with, but he has his place in your life. He does deliver your packages, after all. He is a man. The world is full of these sorts of men. They come in and out of your life. They deliver something and ask you to sign a form. Sometimes they may say something amusing or flirtatious to you. It's meaningless, but these sorts of men can be very helpful to a woman who's lost her mojo. Rather than dismissing every male that walks into your life and saving your smile, your warmth for the elusive Mr. Right, why not go out there in the world and flirt? Smile. Laugh. Treat men as if they are a box of terrific bon bons. You're not actually going to eat the whole box of bon bons, but it's nice to look at the selection, notice the different shapes and sizes, the assortment of caramels and clusters and dark chocolate and milk chocolate, the nuts, the syrupy cherries, the dried fruit, the coconut, the marshmallows. Maybe you'll choose one, but that's not the point here. The point is to awaken your senses to possibility.

And I mean possibility. Not probability.

One Man Begets Another and Another

All right, here's another way to look at it. Men are by nature competitive. They especially like to compete against each other. They always have one eye on what the Joneses are doing. All you need is one to get the ball rolling. The man you flirt with doesn't have to be a love interest at all. In fact, he can be your gay friend. The point is to be seen laughing and flirting and having fun. Men need to observe you with another man or a group of friends. In fact, it's better if they witness your beauty from a bit of distance before they make a move.

Imagine this scenario: You are accepting the package from the UPS guy. You are laughing about the weather or you are complimenting him on his timely delivery or how happy you are to receive this particular package. Unbeknownst to you, there is a man who works near you, observing. You have never actually talked to this man. Maybe he's new or maybe he only visits the company for meetings. But he is watching you, and now as you hand the pen back to the UPS fella, he is coveting you. He is wishing he had a clipboard and a pen and a brown uniform. He is noticing the way your hair falls over your cheek when you laugh. He observes a slight blush. And now he is fantasizing about driving a UPS truck on a hot New York City evening, wearing brown shorts. He arrives at your office and you say something about the heat and he agrees. It's hot out there. The electrical grid is at capacity level, straining from all those office air conditioners blasting, when suddenly, the lights dim, then go on and off and on and then off. And then there you are, alone in the darkness with you and him and the heat and the package.

Yes, this is the sort of thing that goes through a man's brain in the nanosecond he sees you signing the delivery form.

Let Them Witness Your Power

When men get a chance to observe you from afar, it gets their imagination moving. And it's healthy for them to get a little jealous, a bit anxious. Also, they get to see how you interact with another man. They get to see how you behave in your natural world, and they get to see that another man finds you interesting and pleasant to chat with. But what's great about being friendly with someone like the UPS guy, or the clerk at the bank, or the guy from accounting, is that you are doing nothing more than that—you are probably not even aware that you are being observed, so there is none of that dreaded gamesmanship that men fear so much because they want to keep all the game playing to themselves. And even if there is no man observing you being charming and delightful, it's still a powerful way for you to practice your art and get your chi flowing. Just keep the exchange friendly and perfectly innocent.

The idea is that when we are simply alive to our world and the people in our world or work or lives, we are naturally creating sexual chi. Men watch us. And whether we know it or not, we are constantly whetting their appetites. Just by being female we can't help but make them think naughty thoughts. You wonder if that guy who seems to be looking at you from across the subway platform is interested in you. Well, maybe he's not interested in dating you, but he's attracted; he's "filling up his sails" from the visage of you. Perhaps later that night, he'll go home to his wife feeling extra amorous. So ultimately, just by being alive and vibrant, you've done a good deed, and made the world a more loving place.

Start your lessons—for the next three months, you are to go out a lot. You are to flirt—a lot. You are to make men crazy, but no, don't date anyone yet. Just build your confidence. Discover where your power is—maybe it's your smile that makes men nuts, maybe it's the way you walk, maybe it's your gorgeous hair. Don't worry. The men will tell you all about it. This is because when you are just flirting and doing nothing more, you are in a great position of power. Think of it this way: you are shopping and the salesman really wants to make the sale—he'll turn out his best tricks to get you. This is the time a man is most attentive, most focused. So, listen carefully. Take notes on which one of your outfits inspires the most attention—good attention, that is. Men slobbering all over you with their tongues hanging out, maneuvering you into a dark corner for a quickie is not good attention. That's bad attention. Bad! Bad! Bad dog! Down!

No, you want to find out what creates interest in you as a whole person. What makes men intrigued by your body and your mind. This is a subtle art. It means rethinking the fuck-me pumps and going for something a little more discreet.

Take your time. Find out what drives nice guys crazy. This is research and development time for you. Ask a few trusted friends for suggestions on how to play up your most spectacular assets. Then get dressed, go out, and do a test run. And take notes, because this can be a real eye-opener for many of us. You'll be surprised how much attention you can get by being friendly, complimentary, but not really available to men. Married women have always known this—the moment a wedding band is on our finger, the male of the species suddenly becomes more attentive, seductive, and sweet. Why? Because we're already taken, we're nice but we're not available.

So, experiment with being sweet, but not submissive, not available.

This confidence-building experience is really crucial to repair your sense of self-worth. In an effort to sell cosmetics, pharmaceuticals, the services of doctors and surgeons, and a myriad of products, television, film, newspapers, and magazines bombard us with the message that we are not thin enough, young enough, rich enough, pretty enough, hip enough, or smart enough. Basically, we are being told we are just not good enough. And yes, our self-esteem has suffered. The truth is, we are all deserving of love and sex and a good life and we are all *enough*. The media cleverly fuels our insecurities to weaken us into buying and becoming dependent on their products. But men are doing it too. It's a terrific sales ploy—make a woman feel a little desperate, and she'll be grateful for any crumb of affection.

So, here's what you have to do—build your confidence. How? Get dressed, go out, and flirt. That's it. You will make no promises, you will not succumb to a seducer's charms. And if it's driving you crazy, get yourself a good vibrator. That's nobody's business but your own.

Meet Men in Their Natural Habitat

Okay, so where are the boys? They're out there doing boyish things. Most of them are not taking pottery classes or poetry workshops. They're working on a political campaign, they're at a sporting event, they're fishing, they're at Home Depot, they're buying a new car, they're getting their hair cut, they're going to their friends' parties, they're on their way to visit their brother in Seattle, they're taking flying lessons, writing for the local newspaper, trying to hustle a buck, they're in offices, on trains, in the menswear section, they're at church, at the temple, they're shopping for lumber, they're bowling, or golfing, or hiking, they're getting their MBA, their law degree, their architecture license. They're doing manly stuff. They're living their lives.

So now that you know where they are—why not meet them in a natural environment? There's no reason to go to a singles resort or a bar to meet a man. Let's face it. Men go to bars and singles resorts to get laid. You're much better off meeting them in the context of their real world. Better yet, in the context of your real world. That way, they will see you as real, not some fantasy chick in a bikini, available for a good time with no strings attached.

But do get out there in the world. Go to parties, travel, attend conferences, join organizations relating to your work or hobbies, take workshops, classes, take public transportation, go to church, temple, volunteer, get involved.

Ask Questions

When you do see a man you're interested in, ask him for something—advice, directions, even a favor. Many a gal has captured a guy's heart by asking to borrow something such as a map or a pencil. It's a great excuse to start up a conversation, and while the man might suspect you are attracted to him, if you keep the discussion very business-like, completely above board, he will never know. The truth is, men are always having dirty thoughts and feeling terribly guilty about them. So, if you make the encounter about the map or pencil or directions, he will have to push down his baser imaginings and strive to address the issue at hand—the pencil, the map, the directions. Men are incredibly suspicious about being used by women for material goods, so this is the perfect cover for your real motive—to get closer to him. He will have an opportunity to witness your charm, your power, your beauty, but he will never know that he is being very slowly seduced. In fact, if the chemistry is right, he will think he is the one seducing you. Good.

This principle works well with any favor that involves some time together—whether it's walking us to the right train platform or the correct classroom. It gives us an opportunity to get to know someone we already know a little better, and it gives us the opportunity to talk to a stranger without feeling as if he'll get the wrong impression. The key is to keep the focus on the favor and make sure the man in question believes that we are being so nice because we're grateful for his help—not because we're crazy about him. Obviously, we should keep the favor small and insignificant. "I need a kidney transplant. Would you give me one of yours?" is asking too much. Stick to pencils, rides, the correct time, information, and directions.

And a note on safety—truth is, there are some psycho guys out there, so be careful to keep your conversation completely nonsexual. Be wary of subtext and innuendo. Don't allow yourself to be alone with some guy you don't really know. The secret to all flirting is that no one really knows it's flirting. It's just being friendly. But do be smart. Always be subtle.

No Harm in a Little Passive/Aggressive Behavior

Here's another technique for meeting the man you admire. Ignore him. Yes, ignore him. Or, smile at him and flirt for just a moment and then ignore him while you flirt and spend time with another less-compelling gentleman. We've all seen this work many times. It's like this: you walk into a party and you say hello to a guy you really like, you flirt a little, and then his interest seems to wane. He looks around the room, wondering what other hot babes he may be missing while he's spending time chatting with you. You want to punch him in the nose when he does this. The nerve! But rather than becoming violent, move on. Find yourself another man far enough away from the object of your affections, but not so far away that he cannot witness your power to charm. Now, flirt. Have fun. Every once in a while look up and make eye contact with the true object of your affections. Not only will you see the fella in front of you lighting up from all the sudden attention, but soon the first guy will miraculously regain his interest in you. And, generally, men are such unimaginative creatures, so competitive and so desperate to keep up with the other guy, that they will fall for this ruse. Before you know it, the first fella will come sniffing around—and in fact, several more will probably make their way over to you as well. It's that old hunting dog instinct at work.

And if he doesn't—forget him, or turn him into a male friend. Whatever you do, don't take the opposite track and move in on a man. There's usually a very good reason when they don't respond to us—they may have a girlfriend lurking around the corner or a wife at home. They may just not be all that interested in us. They may be secretly in love with a woman in Texas. But here's the tricky part—if we push things, a man will cave in to his inner horndog and sleep with us. But the next day, he's going to get the hell out, because,

"Hey, babe, you're the one who chased me. I never said I wanted something more than a one-night stand." He's got himself a built-in loophole and he probably is embarrassed about the whole ordeal.

Tantric Love Begins Outside the Bedroom

Even when you do have a boyfriend or husband, give him a reason to be vigilant. He should always be concerned that other men are buzzing around. And how do you keep men buzzing around? Well, through flattery of course. John Gray of *Mars/Venus* calls it appreciation. I call it flirting. Either way, it's manna for men.

Men need the sensation of longing and unfulfilled desire, just as much as they need sexual release. We do too. The state of longing builds both our sexual appetites. It creates tension and expectation. When we stretch out the period of arousal—from day to day, ebbing and flowing, letting weeks go by, as he wins some and loses some, and months go by, interspersing union with separation with reunion—the male libido is stirred to attention, because it's the game of love that drives men crazy. It's the drama and intrigue and unpredictability of the pursuit. It's not whether they win or lose, but how they play the game. Look how they love their sports teams, how they follow the ups and downs of the season, memorizing statistics and scores. Whether there is cause to celebrate or mourn, the end of the season always brings a sense of ennui, because for now it's over.

They will spend the off-season recounting spectacular goals and citing specific scores that they've actually committed to memory. This is because men are obsessed with numbers.

Follow the Numbers

This is the key to sussing out where all the men are. Go to anyplace where something needs to be added or subtracted or constantly counted. Go to Wall Street for the money counters. Go to sports centers for the scorekeepers. Go to bridge clubs, chess tournaments, casinos, financial investment classes. If you can stand it, play golf. Follow the money. Follow the numbers. Wherever something needs to be counted, you will find men counting it.

Naturally, the men are crowding up the sciences and the world of finance and economics. But they're also in the social sciences. Looking for a psychologist? Investigate statistical psychology. Want to find yourself a guy who can cook? He's probably shopping in one of those high-tech kitchen wares stores that sell meat thermometers with the most advanced calibration systems. This is true even in the arts. In visual arts, all the guys are hanging out in the photography department—why? Because you have to measure and count, add and subtract. In writing they're in screenwriting, because they like the geometry of the three-act structure, the precise plot points, the guiding rule of one hundred twenty minutes. Performing arts—they're directing, of course, but you'll also find them in administration and fundraising and anyplace where box office receipts are being calculated.

Look for places where things must be measured. How many inches is that fish? Is it as big as my fish? How fast is your car? How many megahertz in your hard drive? I bet my hard drive has more. Is that core sample really two hundred thousand years old? My first book's printing was over four hundred thousand! I've got a V-8 engine. My motor's three hundred two inches. There are seventeen million stars in our solar system. I get forty miles to the gallon. This dowel is a good two-inches thick. My ladder is over six feet when fully extended! I bought GE at thirty-three dollars a share. Do you know how much one thousand two hundred ninety-seven dollars, invested for five years at a nine percent rate of return will yield?

It's enough to make a gal dizzy.

But it does make the search for men fairly simple. Take a look at your profession, where you live, your interests and hobbies, and then follow the numbers. That's where you'll find the men.

Okay, I know, all this sounds almost too simple, too straightforward, but try this: ask a man about his numbers. Ask him to count something, measure anything. You'll see, he'll perk right up. Consider shopping for a motor boat, go to a casino, take a class in investments, go to a vintage car show, take up screenwriting, volunteer at the box office, have lunch on Wall Street, get to know the folks in your finance department or legal division, shop for a new computer, buy some stocks. Not only will you meet men, you'll be out in the world, you'll make friends, and hey, maybe you'll make some money too.

Don't worry about finding Mr. Right. This is not a transaction. This is about being a force in the world. There are plenty of men in this world. More than enough. Think abundantly and do not succumb to the naysayers, the doom and gloom experts at *New York* magazine who only want to scare us into settling for a quickie with a cad in the back of the bar. You're worth more.

Just do the numbers.

chapter six

Build a Coterie

*So many men,
so little time*

> The fact that jealousy sustains desire—or at least kindles it—suggests how precarious desire is. Not only do we need to find a partner, we also need to find a rival. And not only do we have to tell them apart, we also have to keep them apart. We need our rivals to tell us who our partners are. We need our partners to help us find rivals.
>
> —from *Monogamy* by Adam Phillips

Now that you know where all the boys are and you've become an expert at subtle flirtation, it's time to start your collection of men. You'll need at least two in your life, although it's even better to have three or four of them vying for your attention at all times. After all, no one man is going to answer all your needs or give you everything you emotionally require.

So, start a coterie. "What is a coterie?" you ask. It is such an old fashioned word, after all. Webster's defines coterie as such:

1. a group of people who associate closely

2. an exclusive group; clique

3. a group of prairie dogs occupying a communal burrow

I particularly love the last definition, but in this instance, I am not talking about prairie dogs. I am referring to a group of men who are attracted to you and will pay enough attention to you to buoy up your spirits. These gentlemen are not necessarily ever going to become intimate with you, but because you are nice to them or occasionally compliment them, they hold a certain potential, a kind of possibility. They long for you. You do not necessarily long for them. In fact, you may think they are rather dull or unworthy of your time and attention. You may know, in your heart, that you could never succumb to their charms. At least not sexually. In your mind, they are just friends. Yes, you do flirt with them, but you may not have any intention of ever letting the relationship become physical. Yes, there's camaraderie, a friendship, a chemistry. You can have this kind of relationship with an older man, a younger man, a homely man, a man who is just not appropriate for anything serious. This is fine. Building a coterie has nothing to do with anything serious. It's about making us feel desirable. Men we would never consider for a long-term affair or even a short-term affair can make terrific additions to our coterie. They don't have to be contenders.

Keep circulating

The idea of spending even a little bit of time and energy on building a coterie is difficult for most of us. We want to focus on one man at a time—the one that fires up our engines, so to speak, and gets our hearts engaged. We fall in love easily and yes, this is delicious. I am not denying this. All I am suggesting is taking your time, letting desire build, and being cautious with your heart. Really be sure this fella is for you before you become intimate. Too many times we fall into a romance too quickly and we allow ourselves to drop out of circulation. We also allow the man—the new boyfriend or even the husband—to monopolize our time and energies completely. This is a big mistake, because a woman needs to constantly polish and buff and replenish her retinue of admirers. Ask any woman who's gone through a divorce only to look around and realize that all her male friends (and sometimes all her female friends) have drifted out of her life, leaving her isolated with no line back to a single social life.

Even if our love affair or marriage is delightful, after a while we get antsy—especially if our men begin to take us for granted or lose their focus.

The truth is, once we fall in love and give a guy our sex, we have a tendency to take him too seriously. It's easy for us to get too wrapped up in the relationship and this is especially true if we have no other admirers and if we haven't built a coterie to lighten things up when we are feeling needy. The worst thing that happens is that when a romance goes awry, we are truly stranded on the side of the road, and even if we call for assistance—say, sign up for online dating—we find all the men horrid. We get really cranky. No one can please us, and our sense of being light and carefree is gone. This doesn't make us terribly attractive and well, we're just in a bad mood, because we feel we've been "duped again!"

But if you are a wise woman and you have developed a coterie—it's like having a lifetime membership in Triple A. There will always be roadside assistance available to you. There will always be a man who is willing to mend your broken heart.

This is why it's crucial to get out and circulate—even when you are madly in love and just want to spend every moment alone in the dark with the man of your dreams. Fight this urge, and get out and be seen. Men are visual creatures and they can't help but look. So why not use this to your own advantage? Give men something to look at. This is good for the men in your life, and the men in the world. It's good for your boyfriend/husband because he gets to see that you are a force to be reckoned with and that others find you intriguing and attractive. And it's good for strangers to notice you when you're out. Their discreet glances and looks will shore you up, but it'll also serve to put your man on notice: there are others who find you exciting. So find opportunities to show yourself off wearing a great outfit, surrounded by friends and male admirers.

The Myth of the Cat Fight

This creates an air of competition for your affections and will fuel a man's desire. As women, we may find this kind of thing hard to believe or understand. Certainly, when we see a pack of women circling about a fella, we may become intrigued, but as soon as we learn he's "taken," we tend to walk the other way. We really do not want to compete for a man's affections. The idea of the cat fight is a male invention geared to convince us that we are willing to scratch each other's eyes to get our man. But the truth is, we don't generally even want a man who would force us to actually go to battle for him. We're really not into pulling on other women's hair and ripping off their halter tops and calling them "whores and bitches." This is the made-up world of *The Jerry Springer Show, Desperate Housewives,* and *Elimidate,* and it's simple male wish fulfillment and an urge to degrade romantic love. Just read Stephen A. Mitchell's *Can Love Last?*

We just aren't hardwired for this kind of battle, because generally men come after us. Men need sex more than we do and men are willing to do anything to get it. But because they hate this fact, they create all sorts of propaganda to convince us that other women out there are chasing men and making idiots of themselves. We don't have to do that and we never did.

On the other hand, men are willing and actually enjoy the fight. They love the battle. They love sports and keeping scores. They love the unpredictability of football. The surprise seventh inning, the ups and downs of any given season. They actually like running in the dirt and throwing balls and screaming about runs and hits and goals and touchdowns and shouting, "We won! We won!" That is, until next season, when it all starts up again and a new battle must be waged and there will be new touchdowns.

Even the guy who sits on the sofa and spends all Saturday afternoon on his spectator sports secretly covets the life of the quarterback, imagining it is he with the ball, running and chasing and throwing. And the actual real-life quarterback, who really does run and throw and chase and whatever else it is these guys do—he, too, is imagining this is more than a game. He is tapping into his subconscious primitive self. Man before McDonald's—when he had to hunt and chase and kill the wild boar before he could have his Happy Meal.

Why deny men the thrill of the chase?

And, if you don't want to flirt and build a coterie for your own selfish needs, then consider the altruism of giving your man his primal due.

Okay, forget about altruism.

The fact of the matter is, it's hard to build a coterie when one man has "pinned you down." First of all, you've lost your motivation—you're preoccupied, maybe even in love. Truth is, a lot of us have a tendency to immediately collapse into relationships once we've slept with a fella. We like the idea of having our sexual needs met, sometimes even if he's just a "friend with benefits." But here's the problem with this—he's coming over on Saturday night, but is he going to stay? Or will he throw you over—or do something stupid forcing you to throw him over?

Or perhaps you'll decide you'd like more, but it's too late, because you have nothing to bargain with. He's in the habit of coming over on Saturday night with a video and a pizza and suddenly you want to go out to dinner and a nightclub. Babe, we're just friends. And the other evil thought—and don't be shocked, because I've heard men say this—well, if I take her out, my friends will find out that I'm seeing a dog and worse of all, they'll tell my girlfriend. A word of caution: never, ever trust a guy who won't take you out. There's a reason and it's not his budget.

Now, not all men are horndogs. Some are incredibly sensitive. In fact, the truth is, most of them are very, very sensitive. This is why they go through all these hoops and games to keep their hearts from getting broken.

A lot of guys fell in love in the third grade with the little girl with the freckles and sent her a big, hand-made valentine with cardboard cut-out hearts and a white paper doily border with the words "I love you" written in bright red crayon across the top. And you know what the little girl with the freckles did? She laughed. She turned to her best friend Margaret O'Shanahan and the two of them had a good giggle. And our boy? Well, he vowed to never, ever, ever let that happen again.

And so, you are paying for what the girl with the freckles in the third grade did to his fragile heart.

All this is to say, that while you build your coterie and flirt and have fun, consider your true object of affection. Gauge his tolerance level. Always be subtle, and while you're having a good time, be sensitive. No, don't fall into bed because you feel sorry for a guy. But do consider the male ego and be careful. Most of all, be artful.

Take your time, and don't make any promises (either real or imagined) to any one man for a long time. Keep circulating, because the simple fact is that most women aren't in the mood to look for other fellas when we're intimately involved with one man. But men are perfectly capable of two or three or even four-timing. Once they bed one woman, their ego gets all puffed up and they suddenly think, "Wow, I'm the man. I'm on a winning streak. Bring on the babes!" After a while, every time they see you, they begin to envision walls closing in on them and they think, "Oh, my god, this might be it. This one girl. Suppose I end up spending my entire life with her?" (And, of course, there's always the Playboy Bunny possibility.)

His clock begins ticking. So many babes, so little time, and he wants to flee before it's too late!

Keep Your Options Open

I've seen this happen over and over again. A guy is hot and heavy pursuing one particular gal, and then as soon as they sleep together (and it could be on the third date or the three-hundredth date) he loses interest—well, he loses interest in her—and he gets very interested in the wide wonderful world of girls out there.

The answer?

* Don't hop into bed with a guy.
* Don't allow him to take up all your evenings, so that you are in no position to play the field.
* Do flirt.
* Build your coterie.

Now, we're all busy women. We work hard. We're got a lot of responsibilities. And perhaps the time and effort it takes to build a coterie sounds daunting to you. Perhaps you're thinking, "But I just want one guy! Why do I have to make friends with all these other guys when they're not the one?"

Here's my answer to that—if you don't build a coterie, one day, you will wake up like the little piggies whose house is burning down because you made yours out of straw, rather than brick. Your coterie is your fortress. Every girl needs one. Your coterie provides you with flirtations, a place to practice your art, new friends, encouragement, a way to be seen in the world, status, allure, and you never know—your ultimate dreamboat might be lurking around the perimeter of your coterie. So, get busy. Try multitasking. Go to the events/meetings/conferences/seminars that relate to your profession. Look at your life, and the way you lead it right now, and then look at where you might be more social, where you might flirt with men, and find some admirers. The great thing about admirers is that they don't have to be men you particularly like—they just have to like you and give you enough of a cachet that other men will sit up and take notice. The great thing about building your coterie, flirting, and not having sex with anyone for a while is that it makes the whole scene less serious. You'll get your power back, you'll feel strong and sexy. Nobody is using you as their "friends with benefits" while their fiancée is away finishing grad school in Iowa. Nobody is making you wonder how serious they really are. No one is making you nervous and causing you to wonder where this thing is going.

Build a Coterie and Save the Planet

When you build a coterie, flirting with men with whom you have no intention of letting things go anywhere, you'll find that a lot of men will desperately want it to go somewhere. This is good for you. Good for your ego, good for the world. Yes, good for the world. How is it good for the world? Well, let's see, if we don't hop into bed with men unless they're really serious, men will start to realize that if they want sex, they're going to have to get serious.

Think in terms of equal-opportunity flirting. Be sweet as much as you possibly can be sweet. Dress well. Have fun. Not only will we all feel better because we're being nice to each other, but our egos will be built up from the attention—and the tension men begin to feel when their desires are not so quickly satisfied. Nothing short of saving this planet is at stake! Romance, longing, desire, and courtship will even help the American economy because it'll get couples out of the house and into the world, supporting restaurants, bars, cafes, and theatres. No more of this ridiculous "three dates followed by holing up in somebody's bedroom for the next three months until the entire affair devolves into renting videos and eating take-out pizza until finally the gal kicks the guy out because he's such a pig and doesn't ever want to go out."

But, imagine this: we're all out in the world—not so much on dates, but with a group of friends, our coterie—having fun and yes, supporting the economy. Oh, and perhaps walking will come back—just like in Paris we'll promenade down the street, in the park, downtown, because we definitely want to show off our beauty in a public way. Perhaps our town centers will be revived, and downtowns will perk up. People will get in shape from the exercise. Interesting conversations will emerge. Ideas will be exchanged. Great minds will merge! New social projects will be launched! Our communities will thrive and prosper!

So, begin today. Flirt with men. Flirt with girlfriends. Start up a poetic correspondence. Always be gorgeous. Always act as if there is the possibility of meeting someone very, very interesting. Be interested in everyone, in the world. Oh, and please, never, ever start dressing like your husband or husband-to-be or fiancé-to-be. This is death. You are a woman and he is a man. Don't let him put you in a symbolic sack and veil (read: khakis, T-shirt, cropped hair, and baseball cap) as a way of announcing to the world that you are "taken." Never let a man think you're "taken." Guard and maintain your freedom!

The Modern Date Is a Sham

Here's the problem we've created by not building our coterie. We are constantly putting all our eggs in one basket. We go out to dinner with a virtual stranger as if we can honestly judge whether this guy is good marriage material: a potential father to our children. In the meantime, the guy is considering how easy/fun/uncomplicated it would be to bed us and whether we come under the category of a "relationship girl" or a "good-for-now girl." I don't care whether you've been on three dates with this guy or thirty—you don't really know him in the artificial setting of the modern date, which has become nothing more than an on-ramp to the sexual superhighway.

But how do you get to know a man without dating him? How do you find out if he's a nice person, a decent guy, a trustworthy fellow, without dating him? It's simple. You make him part of your coterie.

The Power of Friendship

Make him your friend. Now, don't tell him you're doing this. Men hate the "friend" word because they know this means no sex. But we must retrain them to see that friend means no sex now, not no sex ever. How do you do this? Bring him into your circle. Invite him to the places you go with your friends and family. Be really nice to him, always. Welcoming. Be a good friend. See how he acts with your friends and family. And flirt with him. Lightly. Nicely. This is good for the man's ego and it's good for you. There will be men already in this group, this coterie you've created who are interested in you as well, but they too are "just friends." If their interest has been lagging of late, then this new find will perk them up and make them more competitive. You can never have too many men in your coterie.

Get to know them all well. See how they behave when they're angry, when they lose at badminton. See how they handle their losses in the stock market. See how they treat your friends and family. Obviously, there will be some men in your coterie whom you discover are really not to your liking. This is okay, because you're not going to get naked with them anyway, and it's still good to have an admirer around to attract other admirers. Also, you never know. One of your girlfriends might take a liking to him and even though he's not right for you, he may be perfect for her. So, you see, building a coterie is actually a humanitarian act!

You can keep building your coterie and adding to it. Things only get complicated when you sleep with any of these men. Once you do, you are perceived as "taken," and the other men will back away. After some time, you will most likely know which one in your coterie is truly for you. Then you can let the courtship process begin. Then you can go out to dinner and get romantic. The difference is, you are dating and being sexual with a man you actually know. Someone your friends and family know—not some stranger you met in a bar on Friday night.

Triangles 'R' Us

In his highly illuminating book, *Can Love Last? The Fate of Romance over Time*, the esteemed late psychoanalytic theorist Stephen A. Mitchell suggests that we purposefully create the paradigm of simultaneous safety and danger in our relationships. We need a sense of security, of "home" so that we can then journey outward, test the waters of the unfamiliar, perhaps the forbidden, knowing that we have an established respite of safety to return to when our adventuring is done. Men are particularly prone to this triangle. It comes in many forms, such as the man who has a loving, nurturing wife who bakes cookies and keeps a beautiful home and then a mistress across town who's a painter and has a tendency to throw vases when she's drunk and can't seem to stay in one place for very long. One represents safety, security, the familiar, while the other represents the new, the strange, the adventure, and perhaps even danger. We need both to appreciate both.

The difficulty with love over time is that we grow too familiar with one another and we get into habits that no longer surprise. We grow predictable. It is as if the Yankees played the Red Sox year after year and the score was the same, the players were the same, the fouls and balls and pop flies were all the same. There were no surprises, no tension, no delicious push and pull. Often, we let this happen in our love lives because we want peace. We long for excitement, danger, surprise, and adventure, but we believe we must give this up in the service of calm. We don't want our unions to turn into scenes from *Who's Afraid of Virginia Woolf?* and so we allow ourselves to get captured, pinned down and kept, our girlfriend connections broken, our coteries of male admirers forgotten.

One day, two weeks, or twenty years into a relationship, the man will one day turn to you and say "Why don't you cook brisket anymore?" And you will stare at him, confused, and you will blurt out, "But I've never made brisket in my life! That was your mother!"

Yes, his mother. Chilling, isn't it? But this is what men will do to you. Even the most modern, enlightened gentlemen have a tendency to turn us into their mothers. Why would he do such a crazy thing? Perhaps it is because, as Stephen A. Mitchell suggests, it is difficult to sustain the notion of adventure, the high of unpredictable love-play. And so men (and often women too) create a "home base," a place where they can return knowing that their cuts and bruises will be mended, where there's a warm meal waiting and mama is always there and always the same. Just read Philip Roth's description of his mother in *Portnoy's Complaint*. When a fella turns his wife into this predictable person, this is bad. This is very, very bad, because once you become his "mother," well then he will immediately go into Oedipal Shock Syndrome and he'll have an overwhelming urge to run away from home, leaving behind safety, security, the familiar, mommy, and you.

Men Don't Call It a Coterie, They Call It Being Alive

You may think that no man is going to pin you down this way, but you'd be surprised how sneaky certain men can be when it comes to seducing women and speeding us to the ultimate moment when they must flee from us. In the meantime, this man has other women available. He has an alternate or two or three and so this way he never feels tied down. Even men who have been married for fifty years keep up their flirtations. As long as a man is breathing, he is looking. They may not call it a coterie, but men fantasize about the woman who offers something new or foreign or mysterious or just plain different. Have you ever noticed how a couple will get divorced and within two weeks of the papers being signed, the guy will have already moved in with some other woman? And this isn't because he just happened to meet this new gal. It's because she's been there in his peripheral vision all along.

In this case, what's good for the gander is good for the goose. Your coterie is the best defense against too much familiarity and boredom in your relationship. It keeps the possibility of adventure alive. More than this, a man cannot accuse you of being like his mother or feeling tied down if you are out in the world, laughing, circulating, having fun, and being admired. You are showing him through actions, not so much words, that he does not own you. And no one is being tied down. This will make him want to tie you down. But never let him tie you down (well, you can let him, but it must be for recreational purposes only).

If you're married or have a boyfriend, it's important that you never give in to the temptation to get physical with a member of your coterie. Or if you do, this must be extremely discreet and never spoken of again. But basically, cheating is bad form and will make building and maintaining a coterie extremely difficult because your motives will thereafter always be suspect. So, don't do it. Rather, you should always treat your coterie of male admirers strictly as friends. Yes, friends you sometimes flirt with, but only in a very subtle and nonsexual fashion. All your dealings with your coterie should be absolutely aboveboard. This way, your husband or lover cannot complain when you seek out a member from your coterie for a little entertainment during those times when your mate is not being attentive and needs a little wake-up call, or even when they've gone out of town on business. In Mars/Venus, John Gray describes the phenomenon of how a man (often after a period of intimacy) runs away and hides in his "cave." And while the author suggests a wife go shopping during this period, I have a much better idea. Bring in your coterie! Truth is, after intimacy, we're in the mood for comfort, attention, talk, and the male gaze. We need a little reassurance that we're still desirable, that we haven't given away all our mysteries. So, if your man is snoring in his cave, then it's time to get your chi back elsewhere.

Your Coterie Builds Up Your Ego

Call up the rear guard. This can be one man or several men who are friends (just friends) of yours, but also attracted to you. He's the guy who builds up your ego and makes you feel good. There is an undercurrent of something but neither one of you would ever mention it. (This is why flirting is a lifelong endeavor, because you will always want to add to and refresh your circle of admiring male friends.) This rear guard, this coterie, can include an old friend, a business associate, a gay guy. The main thing is, he makes you feel desirable. Going out to brunch with one or more of these men is much better than shopping for shoes—but of course, if you can combine the two, well, then insecurities be gone! You are a happy girl!

And this will get your boyfriend/husband running out of that cave very fast. That's because, as I've already mentioned, penises have ears. Your coterie is an excellent way to use this phenomenon. If you have a man waiting in the wings, your husband or boyfriend or even the man you have just started seeing will sense that there are others who are ready and willing to take his place. So, if a guy has retreated to his cave, simply get busy with other fellas—he'll come out much quicker this way. This is why it's essential that you keep up your coterie, your flirtations, and polish (or buff) the rear guard.

Love Is an Adventure

Every new person you add to your coterie poses their own landscape, adventure, geography, and potential. Every new man has his own formula, his own history, his own form of flirtation, his own unique language of seduction. The process of discovering this landscape is good for your health. Even in the most delicious romantic alliances, there comes a time when the passion loses some of its original power. Our senses grow a bit dull as we become more and more familiar with one another and even our body chemistry is affected. According to *Psychology Today*, we become lulled into complacency and comfort as our bodies fill up with vasopressin and oxytocin—a neurochemical that allows us attachment and nesting, but diminishes the initial excitement we get from flirtation, romance, and adventure. Helen Fisher, a research anthropologist, says that the problem is that after some time together, our bodies stop producing the neurochemical dopamine. This is the chemical that drives desire, conquest, and makes us feel excited and aroused. So what do you do? You could take on some novel activities like origami or swing dancing. Or perhaps you could take up something that involves an element of risk and danger like mountain climbing. But I suggest simply spending some time with your coterie. Build this into your social life. Show (don't tell) your mate that you are desirable and desired in this world. Get out of the house. Be adventurous. Get those neurochemicals singing.

Creating a Bidding War

And if you are not in a relationship, it's particularly crucial to build a coterie before you get involved with any one man. This is because once you're intimate with a guy it's really hard to find the time, the energy, the will to cultivate your coterie. This is why men give you the rush. When they first meet you, they will call constantly and want to see you three nights in one week. They are working to ensure that no competitors have time to get to you. Then they go in for the kill, bed you, and move on. The key is to slow men down. Think of it this way: you're a real estate mogul. You have this amazing house for sale on this amazing piece of property and you're looking for a buyer. Do you:

1. Ask the first guy who shows some interest to come and live in it free for three months to see if he likes it or not?

2. Fix the place up, paint it, put out some fresh flowers, and have an open house? At the end of the day, close the door, lock it, and wait for all the bids to come rolling in and then choose your best offer?

No, you're not a piece of property, but this is how men are looking at you, truth be told. So be smart. Respect yourself and don't fall for the first fella that comes along. Build a coterie. Let the bids come rolling in.

Men are not terribly original in their thinking. They want what the other guy has. They want the approval of their friends and cohorts. In addition to this, men are at heart conservative, so they do not want what is completely new and never before seen. They want the latest model of something everyone has agreed is just the latest and greatest thing. They are always looking over their shoulders. You know you've seen this—with cars, computers, gadgets. They covet these things not because they truly enrich their lives, but because they elevate their status in the world. Every new acquisition makes the other guys sit up and say, "Hey, look at Ralph and that new Ferrari. He must be doing all right!"

The problem with romance is that once a fella has bedded us, it becomes increasingly difficult for us to remain the exciting new acquisition. It's like this—he has the car a few months, it's in the garage, and it's out, and well, it becomes just another method for getting around town.

When it comes to their relationship with us, we get the same sort of feeling—we're just not as exciting, we're being taken for granted. But if you build a coterie, you create enough intrigue and possibility that he can never imagine he's got you safe and sound, tucked away in the garage. No, you're out. Vroom. Vroom.

This Relationship Can Be Saved (With the Help of a Coterie)

Finally, a coterie offers a reason to keep up one's looks, buy a new pair of boots, lose some weight, go to the Klezmer concert, take up oil painting, and join Habitat for Humanity. While our husbands or boyfriends may lose their focus on us and grow increasingly myopic, other men offer the male gaze. We thrive on this gaze, come alive under its warmth, and as we grow and change, our sleepy mates wake up and come crawling out of their caves to see what new thing we are up to. Ultimately, your coterie is a construction that supports and maintains healthy, sexy, growing, vibrant relationships.

Your coterie are the dunes that protect your coast line, your beach home, your own sense of desirability and worth. Build your coterie. Invest in your future. And protect your assets.

chapter seven

The Art of Resistance

It's thermodynamic, baby

> ❝ War is a failure of mankind to find pleasure in living.

—Sigmund Freud ❞

We long for immortality. And so we long for an epic love, the adventurous life, and a romance that inspires us with delicious memories and warms us as we finally journey toward our own demise. Admit it, you long to be immortalized in story and song. You want epic poems written about your left breast, the flecks of green in your eyes, your pink shoulder, your devastating smile. You want to be serenaded with ballads, to be talked about and cherished for years and years, even after your beauty has faded. You want to be the kind of woman who is spoken about as a force of nature. You want a man's eyes to close when he thinks of you, swept away by the rapture of your touch, shaken to his very core, unhinged, broken, crazed, in love, and overcome with passion. You want a man who sees you as nature herself. Earth, Air, Water, Fire.

Then again, maybe that's just me.

But you know what? That's how men see us—the female—as uncontrollable as nature, as epic as the world, as mysterious as life itself. Wow.

The problem is we're so modest! We say, "No, no, I'm just a regular gal. I'll have Budweiser! Oh, it's okay, I don't need a glass. I'll just drink from the bottle."

This is not epic. This is not romantic. And this is certainly not using all our powers. Powers for what? Powers to create a magnificent, awe-inspiring love affair, something fine and rare and substantial—the kind of romance that lasts a long, long time, the kind of relationship (or marriage, if you like), that men think about on their death bed. Doesn't that just sound delicious?

I will tell you a little secret: it is within your power to orchestrate the epic romance and here's how it's done: Artful Resistance.

Now that you know how to flirt and you've built your coterie, this is your next step. Focus on one man and then simply resist.

Okay, it's a little more complicated than that.

Just as men will do everything in their power to rush you into sex, you must do everything in your power to slow them down, throw them off course, and to sidetrack them. To resist.

How Men Go in for the Kill: Game Theory

The first step is to consider their tools of seduction and examine exactly what they do to get a woman into bed as quickly as possible. Here's how it works: first they convince the customer that she is somehow not up to par. Make her feel insecure. As I've said before, this is done in advertising all the time to great effect. Companies sell us products by getting us to believe we are not beautiful enough, not young-looking enough, not slim enough. Men use the same technique.

It's the Hollywood method of courtship. You bring in some talented, amazing, award-winning screenwriter into the office. Make her feel very comfortable, give her a compliment or two, offer her a Kiwi Sparkler, a Sam Adams, a latté, and then go in for the kill. This means basically making the screenwriter feel bad. "Wow, we really love your script about the woman doctor who travels to Guatemala to bring back her murdered sister's ashes—but it could really use a rewrite. Do you think you could add a little more humor? And how about some sex? Couldn't she have an affair with the guy who murdered her sister? Oh, and suppose she has to get a job as an exotic dancer to pay for her trip! That would sure add some spice, dontcha think? Why don't you go home and do a quick rewrite? On spec of course."

The meeting ends with lots of air kisses and suddenly the virginal screen-writer is walking across the studio lot, staring up at the flat blue sky and the phony sets of Anywhere, USA, wondering why she feels like she just took it up the—well, just took it. But, it's a brilliant maneuver. The screenwriter is given a carrot and the vague promise of some future reward.

This is what our men have been doing to us. First, they flatter, and then they find our weakness, and then using this, they go in for the kill. Because after all—you're not twenty-two, you're not blonde, you could stand to lose five pounds, your nose is not that tiny, your breasts not that big, your ass not that round, your income not that large, your education not that ivy, your neighborhood not that cool, you're not a movie star/lingerie model, oh, and you're not one of the Olsen twins—you're just not that fabulous and you should be grateful for any crumb of affection you can get!

It's the basic good cop/bad cop technique:

Good Cop
* He compliments you.
* He makes you feel comfortable.
* He makes you feel safe.
* He makes vague promises, e.g., One day I'll show you the place on Martha's Vineyard where my dad proposed to my mom.

Bad Cop

* He seeks out your real or imagined weakness or flaw and then criticizes you (sometimes gently, sometimes not so gently).
* He makes you feel vulnerable, not good enough.
* He gently reassures you that it's okay with him that you're not a Victoria's Secret model.
* He goes in for the kill and seduces you.
* Two weeks later he's gone because, hey, you're not a Victoria's Secret model!

Deconstructing the Periodontist

It's a technique men have been using since the Stone Age. It's as old as the boy who dips the girl's braid in the inkwell because he actually has a crush on her, but this thought pains him so much he cannot simply tell her he likes her, but rather he must hurt her. Here's the contemporary version: a gorgeous forty-six-year old actress has an appointment with a periodontist. This doctor is in his sixties and obviously attracted to this actress/patient. So, what does he do—first he compliments her and flirts with her. And then he goes in for the kill. He begins with, "Well, women your age…." and then continues on a doom and gloom story about her diminishing chances for achieving the perfect smile because she must be "at least premenopausal." Truth is, for forty-six, she's beautiful, in terrific health, and in great shape. But that's not the point. The point is, he's using the good cop/bad cop technique—first he makes our friend feel flattered, but then he tries to make her feel insecure about her age. This way, she will be grateful when the doctor—twenty years her senior—makes a pass. And don't be shocked if you're thinking—oh my! That's unethical! Doctors aren't allowed to make passes at their patients! Gals, ask yourself—how many times have male doctors made overt or subtle passes? I rest my case.

Okay, the doctor is not really making a pass, not yet, anyway. He's just working on his game. Most men do this and they don't even know they're doing it. It's second nature. Put down the woman, so she feels vulnerable. Go in for the kill. They do it everyday just for fun and because it's so easy. Often, they actually come across a gal who falls for it and is grateful for the next step in the seduction process, which is where the man says, "Oh, but I don't mind that you're (fill in the blank here). I see the real you. I appreciate the real you. Now how about a drink?" It's so easy for them to pull this one because our media has done most of the groundwork in making us feel insecure that it's not even all that much fun for men anymore. Not really.

But here's what we can do about it. Resist. Don't fall for this trap. Offer interesting resistance. This is what they really want and need—a chase, a challenge, something thrilling and dramatic. Something worth the effort. Something exciting to get their blood boiling.

How to stage an epic romance then?

Well, now that you've collected your coterie, it's time to work it. Try this experiment. Go to a party or a bar with a man or two from your coterie. These fellas will be your "wingmen," although they won't be aware of this fact.

Wingmen and Their Wicked Ways

I picked up the term "wingmen" from an article in the *New York Times* Sunday Styles section. It was originally used in the film *Top Gun* to refer to a pilot's buddy who will accompany him in the air and on the ground—basically keeping a woman's girlfriends occupied so that our hero can isolate and chat up his object of desire. Nowadays, men are actually paying—yes, paying money, real money—for "wingwomen" to accompany them to bars and parties and subtly introduce them to attractive females. The attractive females never know they are being set up. But because they believe this man must be okay—after all, he's a friend of a very nice woman—they give out their phone numbers, date, and probably go to bed with these guys, never knowing it was a setup that cost the gentlemen fifty dollars per hour.

Why the switch from wingmen to fifty-dollar-an-hour wingwomen? Well, apparently, women are much more effective in making acquaintances with other women and introducing a male "friend" into the conversation. And according to Shane Forbes, a computer programmer who started Wingwomen.com, women have "developed reactive strategies to counteract the wingman's pickup mission." Yes, gals have developed defenses. In fact, I've recently learned how college-age girls and women in their twenties use a technique known as "The Cockblock." This is a girl who accompanies her friend or friends to a bar or party and agrees to 1) not drink and 2) make sure the friend goes home with her and her friends and not the horndog sidling up to her at the pool table. Isn't it interesting that it would seem girls still want chaperones? In the excellent book, *A Return to Modest,* Wendy Shalit explains how women's traditional reasons to say no to sex (parental/societal constraints) have all been virtually taken away. This is why young women are becoming more and more creative in their quest to keep the predators at bay.

But now, Forbes says that with the help of these wingwomen, men have a 65 percent "conversion rate," meaning the unsuspecting female targets are converted—so convinced of a man's worthiness that they give out their phone numbers to the male client who paid his wingwoman to pretend they were friends. Truth is, the guy and the wingwoman just met five minutes ago outside the bar/party/whatever. He's basically a John who wants to pick out his own "date." Forbes says that the wingwoman technique works because when a woman sees a man with a female friend she perceives him as "having a seal of approval and being less hostile." There's certainly some truth to this.

When a lone man approaches us, we're a little suspicious. We don't know who he is, really. For all we know, he could be a serial killer just stopping by for a glass of cold Chardonnay. But if he's with a female friend, we figure he can't be too bad. This is why men will pay good money to get us to let our defenses drop. They know that a woman's biggest fear is she'll go home with a brute or worse. In fact, the authors of *How to Succeed with Women* say, "Fear of being abused, hurt, or raped by men is the biggest concern women have in dating." Men know this, so they're willing to hire a nice friendly girl to make them look like they're a good guy, perfectly safe, connected to the community of nice girls and friendly people. But it's all a sham!

You Need an Escort/Chaperone/Wingman

Knowing this, we shouldn't feel at all as if we're playing a game if we bring along a protective wingman. Someone who will create a roadblock. Yes, pick a fella or two out of your coterie and go to a party. Circulate. Laugh. Have fun. Go ahead and flirt with a man, knowing he won't think you're chasing him because after all, you're already with a fella. You're obviously a popular gal. (Just a reminder: flirting is light, subtle, free of sexual innuendo.) But more than this, your wingmen/coterie can play defense if a guy is really a creep.

Here's what's great about bringing along a member of your coterie to a party or bar:

* You always have someone to talk to and be seen with.
* You have someone to circulate with.
* You can be extra friendly and meet men, knowing they won't think you're "after them" because you're already with someone.
* If you end up talking to a bore, you have an excuse and you can exit quickly.

* The guy from your coterie can help make introductions, and small talk.
* He can fetch you drinks!

This is why it's important to choose a coterie wisely. You'll want to collect men who are willing to be your escort, flirt lightly, but always keep a gentlemanly distance. It's a delicate balance, really. There's no room for brutes in your coterie, because the fact of the matter is, men can become dangerous if pushed too hard. Your flirtations therefore must remain extremely subtle and you must never get physical with members of your coterie. And don't get jealous when they date other women. It's their right; after all, they really are just friends.

Resistance=Friction=Heat

However, they are friends who provide you with a kind of counterweight in the world of men. This counterweight provides enough resistance so that you cannot easily fall into the arms of a desirable gentleman. In a way, going out with a fella from your coterie is similar to going out with a protective older brother as a chaperone. This third wheel—this prying eye—poses just enough of a challenge to intrigue the true object of affection. He must work harder to corner you, to get you alone. This counterweight slows his seduction way down. And that's what you want. The fella who's courting you may complain that you're hardly ever alone, but this will cause the necessary friction you need to create real heat. Of course, there will be times when he gets to see you alone, but if you're vigilant at the start of an attraction, this will feel like a rare treat for him. If you are out at a party with your coterie, do be sure to separate and go off alone on some excuse—to get a drink, to go to the ladies room, check on what's happening on the deck, or talk to some girlfriends. Movement and mystery is key. Certainly, you can and should flirt with fellas, but your coterie can then provide you with much-needed resistance when a particular man starts trying to monopolize your time. Don't be afraid that your having other men around will discourage a man. There is nothing like a coterie to make a man feel the urge to push forward. And don't forget the story from *Cad: Confessions of a Toxic Bachelor*. Ilene captured and kept her cad's attentions because she was frequently surrounded by male friends. Plus she had a protective assistant who disapproved of the cad, gave him a hard time every time he phoned, and served as a guardian at the gates to her mistress's lair. This only made the cad more intrigued.

Even when you're married or have a boyfriend, keep up this sense of resistance. This is when a coterie really comes in handy. Husbands' attentions can lapse because they feel they "have you" and now everything is settled. Boyfriends can chafe under the collar of monogamy and begin to lose focus. Building a coterie is not about being unfaithful. It is simply about getting out in the world and cultivating friendships—not just with the gals from the yoga class or the book club, but also with interesting men. Lots of interesting men, who can serve as roadblocks.

You want to create enough roadblocks that you slow down your man. Slow him *way* down, so you can get to know him, so you can become friends and see what he's really like, and yes, suss out all the hidden ex-wives he still sleeps with and the girlfriends hidden away in New Jersey. It's easy to force a guy to slow down when you are seemingly already involved—and yet maybe not. One of the major functions of a coterie is to create a kind of ambiguity concerning your availability. This confusion as to whether you actually have a boyfriend or not gives you a terrific roadblock. With this you create resistance and when combined with his forward movement to get to know you, a lively friction and heat is created. When you are encouraging, but not willing to succumb to the fast-food-sex mentality, you become more interesting. He has to wait. The tension builds. There is power to this; steam is produced—and enough energy to illuminate the entire eastern seaboard.

Okay, maybe that's an exaggeration. But you get the idea. And it's not just men who thrive on this kind of forward motion paired with resistance. We need it too. It creates a sense of sexual aliveness, even if we're married and the resistance is illusory. The truth is, married couples lose a great deal of the heat of sexuality because it's so damned available. You just get into bed, turn out the lights, and roll over. "Hey there, you come here often? Well, actually, yeah, I sleep in this bed, remember?"

The trick is to begin the romance outside of the bedroom. And take your time. Go out where the men (and lively, interesting women) are, and if you're married, go out together. It's crucial that your husband sees you dressed up, out in the world, surrounded by other women and especially attentive men. And if your husband notices and talks to other women—good. A little innocent flirtation will add some wind to his sails and as long as he's bringing this desire home to you, it's a good thing. So go out. It's important that he sees you doing whatever it is you do best, so he knows that you are a force in the world. Yes, he knows at the end of the day, you are going home with him, but he should also feel very lucky about that, imagining as he sees you at a distance what it would be like if he did not have you "nailed."

Save the World from More Stand-up Comics

Whether married or single, a completely satiated man is no fun to be around. They lose focus. They start thinking about things like baseball scores and stock market reports. They suddenly get an urge to try their hand at stand-up comedy. And believe me, you'll want to circumvent this eventuality at all costs. So, stir a man's appetite by being attractive, but not easily available. Be tempting and delicious, but do no more than whet his appetite and then offer resistance. This will make him very hungry and very attentive. This is not to say that sex over time diminishes pleasure. In fact, most married people will tell you that it takes years to get to know each other's bodies and that sex gets deeper and better as time goes by. According to Stephen A. Mitchell, the main danger in marital love is that this very familiarity, this closeness, this deep connection can also pull couples apart. The key to keeping sex alive is to balance this familiarity with a steady dose of adventure, the unknown, the unexpected. The first step is to get your mate to see you with new eyes. Let him know through your actions—rather than your words—that he still has not deconstructed you completely. You are still a mystery. You are still a puzzle and it will take him the rest of his life to figure you out completely and even then, he will never quite succeed. How do you do this? Step back. Get dressed up and go out. Let him see you through other men's eyes. Let him refocus on who you are now, because you are changing daily, and he can never take you for granted.

Getting dressed up, going out, flirting, developing a coterie of men, offering the object of your true desire resistance by not being completely available, but still being sweet and charming—all this might sound like an awful lot of work. But consider the alternative. We see our man's interest flagging. This makes us cranky. We're too embarrassed to say, hey, pay attention to me! Love me! Woo me! Chase me! Compliment me on my hair/dress/shoes/breasts/legs/intelligence! Hug me! Kiss me! Be affectionate! Buy me a trinket! Seduce me again and again and again! And take me to Cancun! So, what do we do instead? We get rip-roaring drunk, embarrass him in front of his colleagues and their wives, beat him up, and finally accuse him of murdering the imaginary son we never actually had.

Okay, sorry. That's from *Who's Afraid of Virginia Woolf?* But you get the idea. We want attention and we'll even start a fight to get it. But, I'm suggesting something so much more pleasant: get dressed, go out, and flirt. This is not about making your man jealous. It's about creating enough distance so that he sees you on display with new eyes. This creates resistance—because he cannot leap on you in the middle of a crowd. This induces sexual friction and energy is produced. Sexual energy. And this is good.

Keep Your Distance

How else can you create resistance? Well, never turn into mommy. Never get so involved in his life and work that he feels he no longer has to impress you because it feels as if you're a blood relative. Remain a little separate. Have your own life, your own interests, your own passions. (And for God's sake, never wear matching baseball caps!)

You should still flatter and flirt with your man (or as John Gray calls it, "show your appreciation"). The main point is to remain separate and resist collapsing into each other. You are a woman and he is a man. Your differences make things interesting and spicy. If you turn into a matched set, well, then he might as well just make love to himself. So cultivate your separateness and your differences—this makes seduction interesting—whether it's the first time or the fifty-seven-thousandth time.

Now, occasionally a member of your coterie may become difficult and begin to push you to become intimate. If this happens, you must push him away. And if he continues to give you trouble, completely distance yourself. You do not need a trouble-maker in your coterie. He may complain, but most people won't blame you for his "hurt feelings" because the truth is, we women have a lot more leeway when it comes to being flirtatious. This is because we are perceived as being basically harmless (which of course we know is ridiculous). But people tend to think that the ultimate act of sexual consummation is the male arena, because…well, because he has the penis and the penis does all the penetrating. And because we are anatomically built to accept rather than penetrate, our flirtations are seen as fairly innocuous. We are seen as babes in the woods or naive bunny rabbits when it comes to men on the prowl. See the film *Swingers* for a dramatic example of this. No one thinks we are really so dangerous as long as we keep our flirting subtle and free of sexual innuendo.

We can't even be accused of being an egotist or scene-stealer if we keep the flirtation to simple smiling and asking nice questions of a man. We are simply being interested. Nothing wrong with that.

Now, if you've been dating a guy for a while, you may be having trouble making him wait and keeping him at a bit of distance. He's probably pressuring you for some kind of intimacy. How do you get him to cool his heels, but keep him intrigued? Don't see him more than once a week. Don't be available every weekend. Turn down a few invitations. Be mysterious. Don't let him listen to your answering machine or read your mail. Here's where *The Rules* got it right.

Don't let him into your home until you're good and ready. Men won't admit this, but the moment you let them into your home, they think they're going to get some.

Gypsy Rose Lee Knew What She Was Doing

Imagine your life as one great strip tease. First he gets to go out on a date with you and you alone, *sans* coterie. Then the two of you go to a party downtown with a bunch of coworkers. When summer comes, you go swimming at the beach together and he gets to see you in a bathing suit. Later, he meets your parents, sees the house where you grew up, and celebrates Thanksgiving with your family. He hears the story of how your younger brother died in a boating accident when you were twelve and he comforts you. You talk on the phone in the middle of the night because you have insomnia and you discover how you both loved *Mad* magazine when you were kids. Together, you discover the joys of melted chocolate on raspberry sorbet. You meet his mom. You learn about the time he won the trophy for playing tennis. One day you walk with him to the back of his old elementary school and go on the swings as if you were nine years old and there, you kiss. And two weeks later, the two of you make love on a rainy Tuesday in November and you never forget it for as long as you live.

This is epic.

And this takes time.

Maybe we have the movies to blame for convincing us that love takes place at twenty-four frames a second and it's all over after one hundred and twenty minutes. But, you know, your life is a whole lot longer. So resist the channel-changer mentality and take your time.

At the early stages of a romance, you do not want to become exclusive, go steady, or "hook up." And there is no reason to, especially if you resist intimacy. So, play the field for as long as possible. This should be easy if you've built your coterie. Now, this doesn't mean you actually have to see the members of your coterie every single week, but you should have some kind of contact with each one of them throughout the week. This could mean a little email or a phone call or a postcard or yes, actually seeing them. The key to juggling three to five men at once is to keep it light and breezy. In fact, don't even let on that you think of these men as potential suitors, but rather treat them as platonic friends. Go ahead and flirt, but never let on that they have any real chance with you. Simply be charming and intriguing. The truth is, they may not have any chance with you.

Dating in the Olden Days

Does all this sound cruel? Manipulative? Mean? It's not, really. It's what women used to do in the old days before equal-opportunity dating. Not too long ago, I met an elegant woman at the Darien Country Club. She was in her seventies—tall, slender, athletic, with shimmering silver hair. When she walked into the room she turned heads. Later, she sat next to me and told stories about courtship in the 1940s when she was in her early twenties. Every night she'd have a date with a new man. They'd arrive at her door with flowers and chocolates and all sorts of little offerings and then they'd take her out for a fabulous night on the town. Then on top of this, at the end of the evening, they'd park on some moon-lit drive in his roadster and court and spark. She said she'd go and do the same thing the next night and the night after that with some other fellow. And she loved it. She was being courted and wooed. She was collecting trinkets and her home was filled with fresh flowers. Okay, maybe she herself was a little sexually frustrated, but I think that's a small price to pay for not being tied down to the one male who "nailed" her. She was free. Things were kept light and delicious and artful. And after a year or two of this dating whirlwind, she got married and is still married to the same gentleman today.

We may frown on this retro form of dating, because many of us have gotten used to the idea of ten or even twenty years of being wild and single and going out with tons of guys and having lots of sex and lots of interesting experiences. And we imagine men aren't going to pay for wining and dining us, not unless they're getting some, anyway.

The Deflation of Our Sexual Currency

Has this system really worked for us? After twenty years of "relationships" (an artless, clinical word if I ever heard one!) we look around and say, "Okay, I'm ready to settle down now!" But guess what? There is hardly any incentive for men to settle down—I mean, by god, there are so many babes out there still to be had—and so they find themselves dating younger and younger women who will not pressure them about a "future" together. In the meantime, older women wake up one day and wonder what the hell happened! Here's what happened: we declared we wanted sex just as much as men and so we gave men sex in exchange for dinner and maybe a show, sometimes less than that. But really, how is that so different from giving them sex in exchange for marriage? Not much, except now our sex has been drastically devalued. And please don't balk at the idea of female sexuality being a commodity. Practically every single product we buy is sold on the manipulation of female sexuality. If you drink this beer, you'll get babes. If you buy this car, you'll get babes. If you take this *How to be a Millionaire* course, you'll get babes. Turn on MTV and watch how music is sold. Oh, and one bare nipple on network television—that's worth a half-million-dollar fine.

It's true that many of us have come of age in an era that promotes complete honesty and communication. We have been taught that if we are forthright and simply tell men what we need and desire, they will be forthcoming. But, unfortunately, men are not playing fair, really. And if you happen to be playing fair, being honest, forthright, and direct about your needs and desires then you're probably a single forty-something woman, sitting on the sidelines, shaking your head as men your age date and marry twenty-eight-year-olds, while you are only getting asked out by guys with hair growing out of their ears. You may even be asking yourself—if a forty-year-old guy can marry a twenty-eight-year-old girl, then why is it you can't marry someone twelve years your junior? Actually, you can have sex with the youngster. Many twenty-somethings put ads in the personals looking for "older women who really understand their bodies because girls my age just don't understand my needs." (Can you believe I actually found this in a personal ad in the back of *New York* magazine?) Yeah, right. True, you could probably have some pretty hot sex with a youngster. Just don't expect him to be around when the *SpongeBob SquarePants* marathon is on cable.

Colette Warned us

And the truth is, when younger men go after older women, it's often because they don't want the pressure of a real relationship. They're just in it for the sex and one day, just like Cheri in Colette's novels *Cheri* and the *Last of Cheri,* the young man will abandon the older woman to marry someone that mama approves of—most likely someone his own age, who'll bear her a grandchild or two or three.

When it comes to the ménage of love, the monkeys have been running the zoo and naturally, they've set up rules that are most beneficial for them, not us. This means a quick seduction, rushing you into bed before you know what's happening, and then making a quick and easy exit—hopefully leaving things off as "friends" so you can go from conquest to "piece on the side." What kind of women ends up becoming the piece on the side? The authors from *How to Succeed with Women* explain, "They may be ex-girlfriends, women who are not extremely attractive, much older women, close female friends, women who understand you don't want a relationship, or married women."

A smart feminist doesn't ignore these facts. A smart feminist deals with them. A smart feminist strives to own her sexuality, to protect it, and to manage the men who want it, instead of giving it away as if it's worth no more than the price of dinner and a movie.

But we want sex just as much as men! Yes, but you will not go to the kind of extraordinary lengths that men will go to for sex. You will not hire escorts. And you will not pay fifty dollars an hour for wingwomen.

Sex has always been free for us and readily available. We have certainly never had to pay for it. The fact is, if all we wanted was sex, we could go out right now and sleep with five men. For them, sex is harder to come by and yes, they're willing to pay for it and many of them do.

The guys make more money than we do, they hold more powerful positions in government and finance and business and the arts than we do, but we have this one thing they need more than anything else in the world. Sex. So, please, don't just give it away.

Let Him Cool His Heels

Here's the interesting thing about making men wait for sex. Only the ones who never win you complain about it. And that's because they're still trying to win you and will always be trying for the rest of their natural lives, right up to their deathbed, which is kind of nice when you think about it. They're the ones who will flirt like crazy when you run into them twenty years later at a cocktail party—still completely enamored and making your lover or husband or the fifteen other men who are lusting after you very, very jealous and nervous.

And the man that does win you over? He will always feel good about the hard-won victory. No, he probably won't admit this to you, but if you listen—really listen—to men talk, you'll realize that they're thrilled by the idea that they've captured the heart of a woman who was not easy. And when I say "easy" I'm not just talking about easy virtue, I'm talking about being easygoing. A nice gal, a pal, a good sport. There's no resistance there. There's no heat, friction, no fun, no spinning their head around and pulling them up out of their rut and making them see the world brand new.

Loose Lips Sink Ships

So, when you are intimate with a man, do everything possible to protect your reputation. We live in a small world. It's a global community and men talk. There's the Internet and pictures of naked ex-girlfriends show up all the time. We may think that the double standard of sexuality is stupid, outdated, and just plain ridiculous—you know the notion that it's okay for men to be dogs and sleep around, yet it's not so okay for women—but the fact of the matter is, most men still think this way. They have two categories—the good girl and the good-for-now girl. Yes, men actually use women to supply their sexual needs (and hopefully cook and clean their homes) while they are often actually looking around to upgrade to something better. This is an unfortunate reality we have to deal with at this point in time. So be very careful about whom you become intimate with—make sure it's not with a blabbermouth braggadocio. Don't sleep with a guy who's going to tell all his friends that he just scored. Do your part to keep things as discreet as possible. This means limiting public smooching. Public displays of affection as innocent as holding hands can often be misinterpreted. If a fella is just a member of your coterie, you're definitely going to want to keep things nonphysical. You don't want other people to think you are taken, because while it's true men are competitive spirits, they give up on a gal once they know she's been "nailed." Never let anyone perceive you as being "nailed." Even when you're married, strive for at least a sense of spiritual freedom!

And if you're interested in marriage, don't say a word about it. This scares the hell out of men. They want to believe that the women they're attracted to are attracted to them, and they are paying attention to them, and they are the center of the universe. If a man thinks for a second that he is simply a conduit to the ultimate goal of marriage and children, he is going to run for the hills. Men do not fantasize about marriage and having children the way some of us do. Most men are not picturing their wedding day or daydreaming about what they'll name their first born. They're not sticking pillows under their T-shirts to see what they'll look like when they're nine months pregnant or playacting the game "I'm in labor, honey! Quick! Get me to the maternity ward!" And they're certainly not sneaking peeks at *Modern Bride*. No, they're looking at

Maxim, Penthouse, Playboy, and *Esquire*. They're reading articles on how to bed more broads. Just take a look at the men's magazines for a little wake-up call. You'll see, all they are thinking about is sex. Sex. Sex. Sex. Sex.

And once they have sex and are satiated, they're thinking about food and cars. And then after that, work—because work begets money and money begets sex and food and cars and so on.

But, we're thinking about a whole lot more. We tend to focus in on one man and one man at a time and we tend to fall in love quickly. We are not great multi-taskers in the world of courtship. We've lost our ancient art of juggling several suitors, resisting their clever ploys to win our hearts, and taking our time while we separate out the wheat from the chaff, the con men from the contenders. I hate to emphasize this so much, but the truth is there are a lot of sexual con men out there: There are guys who just sleep with us to put another notch on their belt, guys who seduce us because they collect nationalities, "Oh, I got myself a Lithuanian girl this time!" The fellas who like to brag about bagging a famous broad. "That's right—I spent the night with Martha Stewart! Boy, is she a hottie!" Men will use girls like trading cards, always looking to capture the illusive and rare one. Girls, be careful out there.

Here are some of the ploys a fella will use to get you into bed:

The Obvious Ones:

1. But I'm only in town for three nights.
2. Admit it, you know you want it just as much as me.
3. Here, have another drink!
4. Come up and see my charcoal etchings/espresso maker/hand-carved African sculptures/authentic 1950s Formica kitchen table/the two stale onions that I have in the bottom drawer of my refrigerator.
5. I love you! I know we just met forty-five minutes ago, but I love you!

The Bullies:
1. Well, you're no spring chicken.
2. You think you could do better?
3. Hey, I thought you were so free and wild?

The Hipsters:
1. You still listen to the Strokes? That's really cute! My kid brother listens to them too!
2. Come up to my room and listen to my new Elliott Smith record. That's right, I'm so cool, I own a vintage record player. Only vinyl for me!

The Poet Men:
1. Well, I just came from lunch with Yusef. Yusef! You don't know Yusef?
2. That's right, the PSA is throwing a little fête for me. Would you like to stand around in a crowd of three hundred and watch me be admired?

The Intellectuals:
1. Well, Orson Welles's best work was really in *The Magnificent Ambersons*, not *Citizen Kane*. Duh!
2. By the way, did you happen to see my copy of Kant?
3. Wanna play chess? Oh, no, I'm not very good at all, wink, wink.

The Money Bags:
1. Oops, I just dropped a hundred dollar bill under your chair!
2. Say, wanna hang out with me this afternoon and watch me buy a new mansion?

The Zen Masters:
1. Snow falling on hills/we are making love in bed/I leave at first dawn.
2. It is natural. Even dogs do it.

Why do men bother with all these tricks? Why do they do cartwheels, tell lies, come up with crazy schemes, try to impress us and bully us? To get us into bed! They know it's not easy and truth be told, they're intimidated by you.

Welcome to the Magic Kingdom

That's because you have what Hollywood movie producers call the Magic Elixir. That's right, you—Woman—hold the secret to life and death. You are the Golden Key, the Magic Chalice, the Pot of Gold, the Ruby Slippers. This is why men go to extraordinary lengths to capture you, have you, and "taste" your Magic Elixir. This is why, too, they run away. It is dazzling and difficult for them to be with the female for too long. Intimacy reminds them of the place from whence they came. Intimacy reminds them of their own beginnings, their helplessness in this world, and their own mortality.

And besides, their mom is a woman!

Camille Paglia says that homosexual men are more evolved than straight fellows because they have turned away from the mother. But I see it differently. I think of heterosexual men as the more daring of the two groups. To be intimate with a female, the heterosexual male must put aside all thoughts of being swooped back into the mothership in order to make love. He must brace himself, put aside Oedipal fears so that he can return to what Joseph Campbell calls the "innermost cave." He must hold in his mind the idea that this woman he is with is just a woman—she is not Woman. She is not his mother. And he must put aside the idea that he actually longs to be swallowed up by her, that he wants to die inside her, and perhaps even be reborn. He must balance all this in his brain so that he can reach his orgasm, and return with the Elixir, which he holds for a fleeting moment before he realizes it has disappeared into thin air. No wonder men have problems with intimacy! No wonder there is premature ejaculation. No wonder men want to crawl into caves. No wonder men must switch their images of us from Madonna to whore, angel to devil, innocent to seductress—as if sex were just one great big pinball game.

But, knowing this—knowing you hold the Magic Elixir, knowing you have all this power—take your time with love. Resist a little. This gives your man much-needed breathing room before he enters your innermost cave. Give him plenty of time, let him get shored up for the Freudian battle, let him come and go and change his mind and change his mind again. Let him find allies and enemies in the great adventure that is called love. The longer you wait, the more thrilling it will be. So, resist, princess. Resist.

chapter eight

How to Succumb with Style

Gentlemen, start your engines

> In the seventies a great deal of ink was spilt on the problem of repression. But the problem of repression may not, in fact, be worse than its opposite. Imagine Portnoy without a complaint. It's all laid out and demystified for him in junior high. Masturbation is only natural, Portnoy. It's the physical expression of yourself. It relieves tension and migraine headaches...It leaves nothing to define yourself against. It leaves no space for Portnoy to be Portnoy.
>
> —from *Last Night in Paradise* by Katie Roiphe

Once we're in the throes of passion, it's very hard to take a step back and ensure a certain artfulness to the moment of surrender. Sometimes we're just caught up in the rapture of the event. There you are drinking cosmopolitans and discussing the joys of authentic French truffles with a food editor from the *New York Times* when he gently places his hand on your left thigh and well, you're a goner. You've lost your grip—tenuous at best—on terra firma and you are sliding fast.

Next thing you know, he's in your apartment—the place you haven't straightened up in the last two weeks, your clothes piled everywhere, and bottles of nail polish in assorted colors strewn about your coffee table, and there's the fridge that contains nothing but leftover apple strudel and a half can of Diet Coke.

Okay, this is an extreme example, but you get the idea. This isn't the best setting for the culmination of a great romance.

On the other hand, for all our demands to be treated as sexual equals, most of us want the man to think that the first time we have sex with him is mostly his idea, rather than something we wrangled him into. This is because we need to be sure that a man has enough attraction for us to sustain forward motion, that he is not going to flip-flop at the last minute, leaving us a little mortified and very frustrated. No, we generally test a man's bed-worthiness by his willingness to pursue us and his willingness to leap through certain hoops to get us into the bedroom. We also want to know he's not faint of heart and that he's an understanding and compassionate guy, in case we have some hidden flaw that might surface only in an intimate setting. So, sometimes we'll—consciously or unconsciously—run him through certain psychological tests. There's nothing wrong with this—it makes absolute sense. After all, we all want a strong, firm, confident male with a whole lot of stamina between those sheets. So, we put him through little trials outside the bedroom to make sure his tank is full of fuel and his engine is in excellent condition.

Despite all this testing, we sometimes forget to prepare ourselves for the grand moment (see messy apartment example). Or, we have obviously prepared so much that there is no real sense of surrender. Condoms? Check! Scented candles? Check! Breath mints? Check! Man's robe? Check! Sex Toys? Check! Whips and chains? Check! Eggbeaters for breakfast? Check!

The truth is we can plan our moment of surrender without it looking like it was our idea at all, by simply slowing things down. In the old days, women had a slew of people who helped with this—from chaperones to nosey older brothers, difficult mothers, demanding fathers, and dormitories that kicked male visitors out at ten p.m. sharp. Today, we have to be more inventive to keep men at bay.

How to Stage a "Surrender"

There are lots of techniques for doing this, but the easiest is the most straightforward. When you find yourself with a man who is cuddling up to you outside your door, kissing you passionately, and you feel the slight grinding of hips, just say, "I'm not ready. I have to go. I think you're wonderful. Goodnight."

Do not have this conversation inside your apartment/house. I'd like to repeat that—do not have this conversation inside his or your home. Once he's inside your place or his place, you've got a recipe for disaster, the makings for a kind of sexual showdown that will not end prettily. Truth is, many a gal has "agreed" to have sex with a man, because not to "agree" would turn the situation into a physical confrontation and possibly rape. So do not find yourself alone in his place or your place unless you are absolutely ready to succumb. No, these initial conversations must take place outside the home.

Now, there'll be many more conversations about this, and he'll want to know why you're not ready. I'll tell you why you're not ready—you're not ready because you're not sure whether he's a brute, a hit-and-run driver, a fast-food sex maniac, or a complete jerk, and that once you sleep with him you'll find yourself in a Dr. Jekyll and Mr. Hyde situation. But don't say any of this. No, you're just not ready. Maybe you don't sleep with just anybody. Maybe you're practically a virgin. Maybe you are a virgin! Maybe you haven't slept with anyone in quite a while. Maybe you're just very cautious. Maybe, as Mr. Ray Porter in Steve Martin's *Shopgirl* says, you've learned that your body is precious and it mustn't be offered carelessly, as it holds a connection to your heart. Maybe we should all admit that our bodies are connected to our hearts, and that the disconnect has created a pandemic of self-abuse. Perhaps if we admitted as Wendy Shalit suggests in her book *A Return to Modesty* that we cannot disengage our hearts from our bodies when we have sex, the cutting, the anorexia, the bulimia, the overeating, and all the other things we do to announce to the world, "My body is vulnerable and I hurt," would stop.

The truth is, sometimes this self-abuse can serve as a way to limit the number of men we become intimate with. It's a new kind of psychic chaperone/guardian we use because some of us feel as if there's something wrong with us if we simply say, "I'm sexually shy and I can't sleep with just anyone." It's as if our body is saying, through this self-abuse, "Look, I'm a little messed up. Approach with caution." It puts a man on notice—if he can pass this roadblock, well, then maybe you can be together. And so, many of us have created some self-destructive tactics to slow a guy way down. Here are some examples:

The Not-So-Good Roadblocks

Addictions

You'd be surprised how many gals use this one as a buffer between them and intimacy. Insisting on stopping a date in order to score some horse can definitely put a damper on things, but more minor addictions such as smoking and drinking can also be used to create challenges and distance—but is it really worth it?

I'm a bitch

Honestly, many women use this one to weed out the non-contenders and to keep men from going too fast. For certain men it's actually a turn-on. But, generally, it's not very pleasant—for you or for the man. "Yeah, so you have a problem with that?"

I'm psychotic

Note, this is different from being neurotic, which can actually be a very charming and effective roadblock. However, being psychotic is overkill. It can mean you date only men who believe in UFOs and read X-Men comics, or you can never eat food in front of another human being, or you have a debilitating fear of sidewalks. Whatever it is, it serves to keep men at a distance—like, on the other side of the planet.

I only care about my work

In certain instances, this can be an effective roadblock, but if you're always busy and not available, and don't even have time for a bit of flirtation, the fella will feel competitive with your work and that's not good for you or your work.

Strange costumes and customs

If you don't know what I'm talking about just go to a Dungeons and Dragons Live Action Role-Playing Weekend. Actually, please don't.

The tollbooth girl

This is the gal who'll sleep with a guy if he's willing to spend the big bucks on her. Problem is she ends up with guys who think of her as a paid escort service.

The secret handshake

Sometimes we create certain habits and unusual hobbies in an attempt to limit our available sex partners. "Hey man, I can have sex with anyone I damn well feel like, but I *choose* to have sex only with people who incessantly make mixed tapes and listen to Mushi-Mushi, an obscure band from Japan that only five other people in the universe know about. They're going to be at The Venue this weekend—are you going?"

I'm too smart for you

You've seen her—the gal in the corner with the nonprescription eye-glasses reading Foucault, wearing a T-shirt that reads: Only Mensa members need apply.

The whore with the heart of gold

She walks like a whore. She talks like a whore. She dresses like a whore. But guess what—that's actually a cover for being really sweet, nice, and highly intelligent. In fact—surprise! She's got a PhD in biochemistry from Harvard. Problem is, most men are so dazzled by the sheep-in-whore's clothing that they never realize there's a real person underneath.

The biological clock girl

This is the forty-something gal who wants to get married, get pregnant, and have a baby in the next ten minutes. Okay, within the next year. Still, she has no time to waste on getting to know a fella and becoming friends. She doesn't really want the *guy* anyway. She just wants his sperm. "Okay, so like I brought this little vial on the date with me, and I was wondering if you could like just go into the men's room with this copy of *Penthouse* and bring me back a little sample?"

The me thinks she doth protest too much gal

This is the gal who has been dating a guy for months, is sleeping with the fella, and is letting him take up all her free time. She's seeing him exclusively and suddenly finds it necessary to make a speech about how she doesn't really want a boyfriend. She warns him not to get too attached to her and that she is really, really, really not ready for love. This wouldn't be a bad roadblock if she didn't see him exclusively and if she were not sleeping with the guy. But the truth is, she's already in way over her head, and oh, by the way, if you're sleeping with a guy on a regular basis, he's probably your boyfriend.

Strict rules and regulations

We buy a book, right? And it gives us the great Tablet of Dating as if Moses came down and said thou shalt not accept a date for Saturday night after the Wednesday of the sameth week. If you like rules, go back to Catholic school. If you want something epic, then use your imagination and make up your own rules.

The ditzy girl

"I know I'm a famous newspaper columnist, but gee whiz, I keep losing my cell phone in cabs! What's your name again?"

All right, so those are the not-so-great roadblocks. Some are really awful, and some are actually usable if they can be modulated. This is because the concept of the roadblock is actually a very good one. So try a less self-destructive roadblock. You may wonder why, if a man is standing outside your apartment door, you can't just say, "I'd love to have sex with you, but I'm not ready." Is that so hard?

Well yes, in this day and age it is, because the presumption is that your heart and body are separate entities. So we do in fact need lots of tools to slow men down.

Here are some ideas to get you started, but ultimately, you should develop your own roadblocks that suit your personality.

Good Roadblocks

You're sensitive

You feel things deeply. You're emotional. You cry, then laugh, then cry again. Sex is important to you. It's incredibly meaningful. You're passionate, and you're just not capable of casual sex. And that's because you're complex. And yes, you're sensitive. This one is very effective because it challenges the man to be deep and meaningful as well. And with the right man, it'll appeal to his instinct to protect.

Keep it public

Another way to keep things from zooming from zero to intimacy is to keep dates fun, light, and out of the sexual arena. Go to public events. Consider working on a project together that will give you some kind of foundation and history of mutual interests such as serving Thanksgiving dinner at a homeless shelter, joining a fundraising drive, taking French lessons, swing dancing, or joining a bridge club. The truth is, men will not suggest these activities to you, because they know they are not entries to the sexual superhighway. It's up to us to create detours and slowdowns. And it's in your best interest.

You're getting over someone

True, you broke up with George shortly after Woodstock, but hey, you're a sensitive gal. The point with this technique is to throw in a simple roadblock that is not too threatening for the guy pursuing you. After all, the breakup was quite a while ago, so your attachment is purely emotional and there's very little chance you'll ever get back together. Still, this one poses enough of an obstacle that you can use it for quite a while. After all, it takes time to heal a broken heart. This way, you can be very, very nice to the man you're interested in, but still keep him out of your bedroom for a while.

You have a lot of friends

You like to go out in groups. You're popular. Oh, and you've suddenly decided to go on a trip to the Bahamas with your friend, Laurie. You're just not all that available right now, but three weeks from now, how about lunch?

You're not ready for a boyfriend

So, you tell him this and then suppose he says, "That's okay, I don't want to be your boyfriend. I just want to have sex with you." Well, then you have your answer. If he's not ready to be your boyfriend, then why sleep with him? Really! The nerve!

You're innocent

Of course this is hard to pull off if you're fifty-three and have been married four times, but even then it's not impossible. It's a matter of attitude. Maybe you're not "innocent," but you're not jaded. You take romance and sex seriously. You don't jump in easily. It really means something to you, because after all, your body and your heart are truly connected.

The timing always seems off

You always seem flirty and sexy when you're in a public place and not really available. Then when you're alone, you're a little distant and cool. Go figure.

Change your looks

This goes with being moody and changing your mind. You can signal your unpredictability by subtly changing your looks, your hair color. Fellas are often a bit unnerved by this, because they suddenly feel as if they're with a new woman and it takes them a while to feel familiar and catch up to speed. They often feel like they have to start the seduction process all over again. This is good for us.

You've changed your mind

As women, we can always buy some time with men by simply changing our minds. Men expect us to be moody and unpredictable, so why disappoint? We have every right to run hot and cold and this is really good news, because it gives us another roadblock. If a man is being much too pushy, then push him back by letting him know you've changed your mind. But it's best not to actually tell a man you're feeling lukewarm about him. Rather, show him by being a little cool, a little less available, and through reconnecting to your coterie.

Intersperse this with compliments and praise. Oh, and please, please, try not to ever change your mind in the heat of passion. That's asking for trouble. And that's why you should take lots of time along the way, so you're sure you want to sleep with a fella.

Tell him you like girls

Okay, I admit this is a tricky one and you probably shouldn't use this technique unless you really are bisexual. I mention it because I've seen a lot of high school and college girls (who are honestly exploring their sexual orientation) use this one to slow down a fella and it seems very successful. Take a look at the film *Chasing Amy* for an example of this.

Hungry for Love

In an ideal world, all these roadblocks wouldn't be necessary, but the problem with the Sexual Revolution is it left us without armor. True, in order to defend our hearts and our bodies, many of us have become strong, but we've also become a little hard and even brittle. And when we finally do find true love, we tend to collapse under its warmth and nurturing glow. And some of us will get clingy and needy and want constant reassurance that we are loved. But, we are basically looking at our man and searching for mother-love. Sometimes, after years of independence and stamina and steeling ourselves against the vagaries of the workaday world and single life, we feel like empty vessels endlessly needing to be filled. And yes, this frightens men.

This is especially true of women who have or had cold or distant mothers, who grew up not feeling truly seen and loved and emotionally nourished by their mothers. These gals grew up with a deep hunger for love, warmth, and touch.

But, if this is your situation, rather than seeking this kind of love from a man, consider getting your fill of compliments and reassurances and mother-love elsewhere. Look at *Sex and the City,* and how these women "mothered" and supported one another. This is what made the show so successful and so popular—the women's relationship to each other was the primary constant. They shored up one another, laughing and crying and helping each other. This was the true romance on the show and the men were simply comic relief. We loved *Sex and the City* because it authentically showed how women connect and nurture each other. *Desperate Housewives* may be compared to *Sex and the City* but it is not the same. It is male revisionism for network television. The women have no real love for each other. They fight and compete over men and engage in cat fights—a favorite male fantasy. Carrie, Miranda, Samantha, and Charlotte would never do this.

So, how do you fill up on mother-love so you don't approach the bedroom starving for touch and attention? Here's how:

* Cultivate your girlfriend relationships.
* Go shopping.
* Visit your mother!
* Get a massage.
* Get a manicure/pedicure/facial/waxing.
* Buy shoes.
* Spend some time in a sauna.
* Take a yoga class/dance class.
* At least call your mother!

Put Your Boy on a Diet

Now, all this effort, all these machinations, all these roadblocks, detours, and slowdowns might seem like a lot of work to you. And at some point you might be saying, "Damn, I just want to have some quick sex!" I understand this. But here's the deal—we can have sex—that's not so difficult. But there's something else we want just as much as sex. And that's attention. Just as men thrive on praise, we thrive on attention. And men are most attentive when they are after sex. Therefore, we must manage their intake. I know this sounds like a big pain in the neck and we may say, "Hey, can't they manage their own intake? Can't they get just enough sex to satisfy, but not satiate so much that they have to crawl into caves?"

And if you're in your late forties or early fifties or beyond, some of this is going to seem very futile. You've lived through the past thirty-five years of the Sexual Revolution. You're not a kid and resisting now may seem like closing the barn door after the cow has long escaped. But be Zen, because the cow is just lying in the pasture getting fat on clover. Trust me, eventually, it's going to rain. In fact, if we all embrace the idea of resistance, the fat cow is going to come back only to find that the door is closed and the barn has been thoroughly redecorated and he'd better wipe his feet on the doormat before entering.

Start a quiet resistance.

Wait for rain.

He will come.

In the meantime, practice your art.

A Case for Resistance

Not too long ago, I spent a month on an island off the coast of Maine with a group of artists and I witnessed the blossoming romance between a painter and a writer. This painter—let's call her Sally—was brilliant at driving men crazy.

Actually, she was brilliant at romancing one man, in particular—the writer. They were both young and good-looking and clearly interested in one another. The writer fella—let's call him Sam—hovered around her as she cooked dinner wearing a very retro but sexy apron. He made lots of clever remarks, brought in cool CDs to play, and generally preened. In the evening, they got into an arm wrestling match and Sally won. There was a lot of laughter and blushing. One afternoon he did something no one else—not even the most macho men on this island—dared to do: he jumped into the frigid Maine water. Sally was duly impressed. Later, he amazed her by cooking lamb stew. Then, on Friday afternoon, when we all traveled to the mainland, Sally bought a pair of strappy, heeled sandals—completely impractical for the island, but brilliant for catching the eye of her object of desire. She wore them on the boat back to the island. Later that night, everyone got a bit drunk on good wine and while some of the residents went for a midnight walk on the trail in the dark with flashlights, Sally and Sam did not join the group. The next morning, we heard the rumors. They had spent hours on the water in the little row boat with Sam crooning songs as he paddled under the moonlight. Love was clearly in the air, as well as lots of sexual tension. Something was about to happen. Sally spent all day Saturday lying in the sun in her tank top, looking grand, eyes closed, while Sam hovered about, just out of sight. You would think that night would be the big event.

But, no. On Saturday night she disappeared. She had had too much sun, and she needed to retire early. Sam was left out in the cold, filled with longing and desire.

Sam was smitten. And you know what? Sally orchestrated the whole thing—whether she was even conscious of it or not.

Let's deconstruct what she did. First of all, she created a sense of contrast between her and Sam. She was girlish and feminine, but she did it with a wink and a sense humor. She even pulled off wearing those strappy sandals in the frigid Maine air. But she was no slacker. She worked hard at her painting, she was accomplished, and she showed that she could be a regular gal, a slight tomboy especially when she beat him at arm wrestling (prettily, I might add). She showed herself to be an awesome cook and an admiring companion. The rest of us might have thought Sam's leap into the water was an act of insanity, but not Sally. She praised our boy. (John Gray would be proud.) She was friendly to all the island residents and she flirted with everyone—but so subtly you couldn't accuse her of leading anyone on. She was just nice. The most "showing off" she ever did was on the day she sunned herself on the deck in her tank top and shorts. But this bold act was followed by a hasty retreat and a pretty pronouncement that she was feeling faint from having too much sun and had to lie down in her room. She disappeared while Sam kept close by in the common rooms.

So at a point where one might expect a "climactic moment" between Sam and Sally, there was none. But his interest was not diminished. Rather, it intensified.

What did Sally's retreat do for her? It created an air of vulnerability. Not weakness, exactly, but vulnerability. Before we get upset by this word, let me say this—aren't we all vulnerable, really? To fall in love, don't we need to be vulnerable—physically, spiritually, emotionally? Men will readily admit to their vulnerability with women, but for some crazy reason, a lot of us like to deny our own vulnerability. Maybe because it is so undeniably true: we are vulnerable.

And you know what—men know it too.

So why hide it and pretend it doesn't exist? Instead, use your natural vulnerability to slow down the seduction process and stage a great moment of "surrender." No, not complete surrender—never completely surrender—but a little surrender goes a long way in constructing an artful romance.

Imagine this: You've become friends with a wonderful man. He's part of your coterie. A favored fellow. He's seen you in good times and not-so-good times. He's pursued and courted you and been made to wait an excruciatingly long time. He understands why you haven't been ready to be intimate with him because you've used an effective roadblock—either one listed here or one that's specific to you. Now you're ready to consummate the romance (oh, and if you're the type who wants to wait until you're married—there's nothing wrong with that, but just make sure the fella knows this early on).

No Breaking the Fourth Wall

And now, you want to stage the grand moment.

But, you don't want him to know you've staged it. You want him to think you finally could no longer resist his magnificent charms. You want him to think you have not had many lovers. You want him to think he is very, very special. And, if you make men wait an excruciatingly long time to bed you, you honestly won't have had many lovers in your lifetime, because you care more about quality than quantity. And he will be authentically special to you, because you don't sleep with just any old schlub that comes along.

Oh, and the whole AIDS/STDs discussion—that took place long ago in the course of a friendship in an honest moment (not when he's so aroused he'll tell you anything to get into your panties). By now, you know this man. And you are making a conscious decision to become intimate.

But still, he should be kept under the illusion that you succumbed to his passion. How do you do that?

Okay, you begin two to three weeks before the big night. You pave the way by revealing more of yourself. Perhaps you tell him about some sad childhood memory. You let kisses linger longer than usual. You allow a little more sexual innuendo to enter into late-night phone conversations. Generally, you allow things to heat up. You let go of the roadblocks, but you do not succumb, not yet. Use this time to get ready. Clean your home. Make it a sexy place (but nothing so obvious that he'll know you prepared for his arrival). Buy a great dress. Get ready. If you have done your preparations and then you let down your guard—one night, when you just happen to be wearing that gorgeous dress (and your best lingerie) he will take you out. You'll feel the energy in the air all night long. If you've waited long enough and if you really know your man, you'll recognize this erotically charged moment. He will kiss you goodnight and you will breathe and sigh deeply. You will kiss him back with much more abandon.

And he'll know. And you'll know. And it'll be delicious. You will succumb with style and wit and charm and this man will be a great lover. Why? Because you made him feel special. Worthy. And because he knows you. And you know him.

And if you're not a romantic, here's the basic formula:

His Forward Motion + Your Resistance = Struggle
Struggle + Your Kindness/Flirtation = Anticipation
Anticipation + Struggle = Increased Tension/Heat
Increased Tension/Heat = Increased Forward Motion
Increased Forward Motion + Tension/Heat
= Final Surrender + Great Sex.

Epicurean Romance

Now, it may be true that the first time we have sex is often not the best. Nonetheless, the first time is important in setting the parameters of the romance, because it establishes a style from the start. If you want a fast-food affair—where you meet on Wednesday, have sex on Saturday, and break up by Monday, fine. But if you want something more substantial, the first time you become intimate must be preceded by a big investment of time and effort. We always remember the first time we're intimate with someone. You want the man to remember this as his great heroic moment in which he fought the good fight and won the fair maiden. You want him to know he won you through his brains and brawn. You want him to believe he captured you only by being incredibly clever and sexy and intelligent and gentle and strong and wise and funny and brilliant and kind and generous. This way, he will know that if he stops being all those things, he will risk losing you. So, teach your man from the beginning. He's lucky to have you. And if he stops being clever and sexy and intelligent and gentle and strong and wise and funny and brilliant and kind and generous, well then he's going to be in a whole heap of trouble!

Seriously, when we appeal to the best part of a man, he will give us his best. And you in turn will give him your best. And shouldn't sex be like that? Each of us giving our best? Taking our time? Let's make love like gourmands. Make sure the temperature is right. The oven has been preheated. The ingredients are fresh. The flavors blend well. The taste is something close to earth-shattering. Believe me, once you've succumbed to sex with style, you will never go back to fast-food sex.

PART THREE

Advanced Lessons

chapter nine

stick shift Theory

Every man has a stick.
Or shtick, as
the case may be.

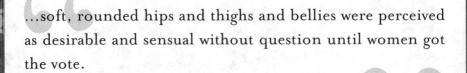

For every action, there's a reaction. That's the law of nature. So, while we were developing our "roadblocks," men haven't been sitting idly by, scratching their heads, and wondering why women are so darn difficult.

Actually, that's not completely true. They have been sitting around wondering why we're so darn difficult. Read their books and you'll hear them complain: if women say they want equality, then why the hell can't they approach us first, ask us out on the date, pay the tab, and seduce us! Honestly, this is what men are really saying. They shake their heads and ask why are women so fickle. Why do women say one thing and then go and do another, they ask themselves.

And we're a little confused too. We may ask ourselves—especially if we came of age during the Sexual Revolution—if we want sex the same way men want sex (read: quickies, sex with strangers, sex without love, casual sex, and friends with benefits), then why have many of us backed away from the whole scene? Why have so many of us created good and not-so-good roadblocks? Why do so many of us insist that the man call us first, ask us out, make the plan for a date, pay for the date, and make the first sexual move?

I'll tell you why—it's because when it comes to sex, we want different things. Yes, we're equal—but we are different. We don't want to just have sex (and believe me, this is it for many men). We want a whole lot more. Yes, we want sex, but often only under certain circumstances. We want to feel special, appreciated, admired, singled out, paid attention to, and understood and we want it with a sense of style, ambience, good lighting, excellent set design, and great costuming! We want a guy who's going to be nice to us the next day, stay for a while, compliment us some more, call, take us out again and again, and say I love you. That's why we create roadblocks. And for some of us, who've been burnt by one too many horndogs, these roadblocks have turned into virtual fortresses.

The Magical Stick (or Shtick)

And yes, men have been doing a lot more than sitting around scratching their heads and asking why women are so difficult. They've taken note of our roadblocks and in response, they've developed their sticks. The stick is whatever a man uses to knock down our roadblocks and fortresses and shift things into a higher gear. The comedians, the jokesters, and the guys who's main talent is chatting up a gal have developed a shtick as their stick, but basically it's all for the same purpose—to break down any roadblocks in order to make a gal feel vulnerable and insecure and then quickly get her in bed.

Without his stick or shtick, a man is lost. It is a kind of divining rod for the male of the species. But more than this, it's the thing that gets his engine out of first gear and into fourth. It controls the transmission and modulates the power of his thrust—whether he wants to go slow or fast or keep it in neutral. The stick is everything to a man. Without it, he cannot operate in this world. It is his most prized possession. Basically, it's his phallus.

Of course we don't see men ripping open their trousers all the time and announcing "Hey, I have a stick!" Or stripping off all their clothes, like Jackson Pollack famously did, at Peggy Guggenheim's well-attended cocktail party and peeing into her fireplace. No, generally, men try to resist the urge to show off in this fashion. Nonetheless, the desire to do something very untoward, involving their penis, is always with them. But because society frowns on this sort of male exuberance, men must suppress themselves and find alternate forms of expression.

They invent products such as leaf blowers. The remote control. The Club car lock system. The traditionalists like to stand around the barbecue with a long-handled spatula and poke at meat. Professors like to get out their stick and tap at the black board to make a point. Then there are pool players and police officers with their billy clubs, guys who like to hike with their walking sticks, and of course baseball players. Look around. Everywhere you go, you'll find a man with stick. From the beginning of time, men have been using sticks.

How About a Little Poke?

Stick Shift Theory works like this: first, a man will poke around to determine our sensitive spots. This could relate to any aspect of our lives, from our looks to our work to how we organize the books in our bookshelf. Once he's figured out our sensitive spots, he'll take out his bag of sticks and choose one that seems especially suited to hit a line drive.

Here's an example. Recently a friend of mine—a distinguished Yale University professor—went on a first date with a political journalist. He was nice enough to her, but then halfway through the dinner he asked her, "So, how does it feel to be so low on the totem pole at Yale?" I admire my professor friend for keeping her cool and not giving him a hard slap across the face. The nerve!

Of course, there will always be someone above you on the totem pole of life. But to deconstruct this question further, isn't it an interesting concept—this career totem pole—a kind of stick—in which she is either above or below someone else? Never sideways, but always up and down. But this is how men see their world. And the gentleman on the date—he was simply using his stick to subjugate her a little. The intellectual/career stick. This is the second step in Stick Shift Theory. He uses whatever he perceives to be his strength or stick and uses that to bop her on the head. Most men are not so brutish that they would actually hit a woman, so they develop alternative methods of pummeling us into submission. This can range from their superior grasp of a particular political situation to their knowledge of the intricate workings of the human genome to their uncanny ability to deconstruct Kant. The stick a man uses may vary according to the woman he wants to seduce or overwhelm. Obviously, some women are easier to pummel than others. Strong, accomplished, intelligent, successful women who are at the height of their power tend to intimidate men. Sexually confident women can even overwhelm them to the point where they must run away or refill that Viagra prescription post haste. In fact, according to an article in the *New York Times* Sunday Styles section, men are taking Viagra "not for impotence but as insurance against performance anxiety." A gentlemen who takes Viagra is quoted as saying, "There is an increased anxiety among young men because this generation of women is more open to erotica, more articulate about their own needs."

Why Men Retreat

Poor guys are really running scared. No wonder many of them are staying at home, glued to their computer or big screen TV, hypnotized by the warm glow of pornographic images flooding their living rooms. What safety they must find in chat rooms where they can talk dirty but not actually be expected to perform. Is this because we've taken away their sticks and created our own real or metaphoric strap-ons, announcing I'm just as sexually voracious as you, babe— maybe more, so bend over!? Sorry to be so graphic, but you get the point.

So, despite some bad behavior, men still need and deserve their sticks. And truth be told, we like men with good sticks.

I know a gal who's a lead singer in a rock band. She's a force to be reckoned with, this gal. She's tall, blonde, gorgeous, and strong. One night she found herself with another famous rock star. They were alone in his apartment. They ended up on the floor, kissing passionately, whispering, sighing. In the middle of all this, she whispered, "Move your leg," because apparently it was placed uncomfortably on top of her leg. It was a very practical matter. But he didn't hear her correctly and he thought she said, "I'm afraid." Well, he immediately slowed down, became much more attentive and gentle and much more amorous. He stopped his forward motion and talked to her all night. It was truly soulful. And when they finally did make love many days later—according to my friend—it was really spectacular. He was quite the man—gentle, but strong. Powerful, assured. A terrific lover. All this because he imagined she was "afraid."

My friend had actually stumbled upon a brilliant little roadblock. No, she didn't mean to say, "I'm afraid." But what a lovely moment for her and what a beautiful response. And you know what, aren't we all truly a little afraid the first time we sleep with a man? And if we're not, shouldn't we be? Isn't sex with a new person a little scary? We're getting into something unknown and we have no idea what it'll be like, exactly. Every person is so different when it comes to intimate moments. There is so much that goes into our sexuality— desire, fear, hope, dreams, childhood fantasies, the first person we ever lusted after, the way our siblings treated us, the teacher we had the crush on, the first time we looked at pornography, the way an ordinary moment—say watching the sheets on the clothesline sway back and forth, undulating in the breeze—can become deeply eroticized. All this and more goes into creating the roadmap to our sexual psyche. And sometimes, that's scary.

But, I guarantee you this—it will be less scary if you take the time to get to know the man first. If there's some shared history and friendship, then our succumbing has style and grace to it and more than this—it's authentic. Yes, authentic—because when we jump into bed with a virtual stranger (a guy we've known only under the artificial confines of the modern date), we are not really fully engaged in the experience. It's like you're standing in the frigid early June air at the lake in Maine, holding your breath, bracing yourself, and jumping into the very frigid water. A part of your brain is switched off and removed from the experience. When it comes to sex, it's natural to protect our emotions, to hold back a bit, to dive a little half-heartedly, simply because we have grave doubts, and yes, we are scared. Scared for our hearts. Scared for our bodies.

This is the truth. And stick shift or not, men are scared too.

Sex is scary. And love is even scarier.

Tainted Love

In *Can Love Last?*, Stephen A. Mitchell explains that love over time does not automatically become routine and boring, but that we purposefully degrade romance because we are all deeply conflicted by security and sameness. We long to possess our lover and yet, this very possession drives us into a state of panic where we must get away and declare our independence. Men will try to possess women and women try to possess men. Ultimately, no person can possess another. And this is good news. The complexity and contradictions of love are the very things that keep it alive and viable. And yes, scary. Scary is good.

And you should be scared.

Men are certainly scared of us. They know we have incredible power over them. They want our sex desperately and yet, they sense that once inside of us, they are in mortal danger of being swept back into the Oedipal netherland. For them, sex is fraught with peril. This is why they try so hard to separate love from sex. In Pedro Almodovar's brilliant film, *Talk to Her,* you see a rare visual depiction of male love teamed with sexuality. As a story within a story, a chubby man falls in love with a beautiful woman, but he begins to shrink in size, growing smaller and smaller as their love progresses, until finally one day he is so tiny that he enters her vagina and disappears forever. This is what men desire and fear: to enter us and never come out.

Now, knowing this, don't you think they deserve to have their stick—at the very least!

Think about the rock star friend. She unintentionally gave her man the Strength Stick. Not simply the stick of brute strength, although that was part of what happened, but she gave him the stick of emotional strength. By seeming to say, "I'm afraid," she made him feel strong and powerful. As a result, he slowed down and treated her with great kindness. He was strong and gentle. He became protective. And when they did finally make love, there was more of an investment—in time and emotion.

Why not let a man feel strong and powerful? Why not give him his stick? Letting a man feel strong and powerful should not diminish our own sense of strength and power. And it shouldn't feel like a lie. It should feel natural. After all, don't you like to hear that you are beautiful, sexy, appealing? Men like to hear they are strong and powerful or wise and brilliant, talented and adventurous. This isn't about lying. It's about being nice. Men like to know that you appreciate the fact that they're different. They have a penis.

It's Good to Find a Hard Man

Here's a fun fact: the penis wants to penetrate. Perhaps this is why we sometimes have a hard time being nice to men, complimenting them and making them feel strong and powerful. Perhaps we're a little scared of the penis and its powers to penetrate and this is why we resist praising a man's "stick."

Now, maybe we don't care about being penetrated. Maybe we think intercourse is an anachronism from the era where we were concerned with populating the planet. Or perhaps we decided hey, I only orgasm from direct clitoral stimulation, so what do I need intercourse for?

Nonetheless, despite all the emphasis these days on oral pleasure, most of us do want an erect man. We see a man's erection as a sign of his desire for us. Even if our sexual satisfaction is not dependent on a man's erectness, we still want it and need it in order to feel truly aroused. And, after all, we do have a vagina and the vagina wants to be penetrated. We do not want to be penetrated by a half-hearted Wimpster guy who is conflicted about his own orientation and really only thinking about whether it's time to trim his goatee or not. We want to be penetrated by a confident, strong, firm, purpose-filled man.

Here's the problem—if we break down our men's sense of confidence, the penis is not going to be as responsive and the sex is not going to be as delicious as it should be. We need our men erect, but erectness is not simply an erect penis. Erectness is a state of mind. It is psychological, emotional, and yes, physical.

It's All About Power

Today, men are truly scrambling to find their erections. They are taking Viagra for confidence-building; they are meeting women over the Internet and having meaningless one-night stands. And some are so scared of women who are their equals in age and accomplishments that they find refuge in gals who are twenty years their juniors. And contrary to what they'll tell you, they don't go after younger women because they're so darn fertile. If that were truly the case, then they would be attracted to fleshy women with big childbearing hips. And they'd be getting them pregnant! But no, our men with shaky sticks go for younger women because they are not intimidated by them. These younger women have less experience, less money, less power. Therefore, our older man has more experience, more money, and more power—and a big stick! This makes men feel great. These young women look up to older men, they appreciate their power, their money and they even listen to them lecture about the history of rock 'n' roll as if Mick Jagger made his debut only yesterday.

Of course, young women are attractive and help elevate men's status with other men. Men desperately need the approval of their peers. The trophy wife and arm candy can certainly bolster a man's status, but this isn't about youth, because a famous woman, a beautiful older woman, and a very wealthy woman can also elevate a man's status. Still, a young woman builds up his stick like no other woman around, because she makes him feel smart, successful, and yes, superior.

And why is the young woman attracted to the older man? It's more than a father-complex, because if this were simply the case, she might go for any older man, but the older man is usually one with money. She is looking for an older man who can care for her, make introductions and connections, and help with her career. We generally don't make as much money as men, and we risk a substantial loss of income when we marry and have children and oftentimes must take a leave of absence. Men are just as much aware of this as we are, and they know that money is a great source of their power. They will complain that women just want them for their money, but they also know it's an incredible stick for them. Perhaps this is why certain backward-thinking men try to keep us from earning equal pay for equal work. They know that this is another form of eroding male power. And for older men, whose sexual prowess may be waning, money and its force in the world becomes paramount.

And this too is why older men will shy away from women their own age. Forty and fifty-something women have discovered their sense of sexual entitlement. They are more in tune with their desires and needs. They are less concerned with pregnancy and more concerned with sex. And rapture. They make demands. They have an erotic history that has had years to evolve, and perhaps this scares our men. A younger woman has less history; is more malleable and more of a blank slate. She can be molded, or so a man thinks, and this above all else makes him feel powerful and erect—if not literally, then metaphorically.

The simplicity of Stick Shift Theory is actually good news for women. Think about it. Men need to feel powerful, respected, accomplished, and admired. Men need a stick. Is this so terrible? Why can't we just bat our eyelashes, let out a girlish sigh, and tell our man how very powerful he is? Truth is, we find this appalling, hypocritical. Why? Because we fought long and hard for equality and it seems just plain untoward for us to turn back the clock on decades of hard work and look at our men and say, "Oh, you big strong handsome hunk! I am so insignificant and downright dumb compared to you! Please, tell me what to do? Should I put my left shoe on my left foot and my right shoe on my right? Or is it the other way around?"

The Appeal of the Lingerie Model

No, we can't do it. So, we sit on the sidelines and shake our heads while our men drool over the Victoria's Secret catalog. What power do these girls hold over our men? Why are they considered beautiful?

Well, first of all, the Victoria's Secret model doesn't talk!

She lives in her underwear, as if she just happened to be caught in a state of *dishabille*. She never shows everything and so she remains slightly innocent. After all, there are still hooks to be unhooked and strings to be unstrung. She's like all women, he thinks—she wants him to buy her things, but not a new computer, a car, or a condo. She just wants new lingerie and other such delightful fripperies! She is not worried about next month's rent. She does not want to discuss her health insurance situation. She is not naked, lying on the bed, demanding satisfaction—get down there and make me come, now!

And she is not available. I'd like to repeat that. She is not available.

She is a pretty Christmas present, all wrapped up, shiny and new, just waiting to be unwrapped by the right man, who says or does or buys her the right thing. And most important of all, she's a picture in a magazine.

She has no history.

She doesn't have a sink full of dirty dishes.

Her ex-boyfriend isn't in jail.

Her father didn't abuse her.

And maybe all that explains why the poor gal is in a happy delirium, prancing around on a beach in her skivvies!

You get the idea. She is a very pretty, seemingly available, but really a completely unattainable blank slate. She is a fantasy. She will never wear out. She will never demand anything. And she will always be there for the man on the pages. She is his ideal woman! She is the Stepford Wife of the new millennium.

Now, you may ask, how can we compete with that?

How can you even ask that question?!

Of course we can compete with a picture in a magazine! We are living, breathing, lusty, complicated, and interesting women. The reason the Victoria's Secret model is so appealing is because our snakes—I mean, our men—have been lulled into the assumption that they can always get real sex when they want it, but they wonder if is it worth all that work.

Let's be honest. We expect a lot from men these days—especially in the bedroom. We want our orgasms! And too bad for the guy if it takes an hour and a half of heavy licking. Get to work, buddy!

It's Time to Be Nice to the Magical Penis

Our men are exhausted and scared. No wonder they've retreated to pictures. But here's the good news: if we slow down and are not so readily available and not so demanding, we can coax them back. We need to show men that we want and need their penis/stick/power/thrust. We need to let them know that despite the fact that we generally only orgasm through clitoral stimulation, we still honor the stick.

Because the truth is, men are beginning to wonder about this. They're beginning to feel that their penis is an obsolete accoutrement from a bygone era. We don't need the penis for orgasm and we don't need the penis to get pregnant. Perhaps this is why images of spanking have jumped out of the porn arena and are cropping up all over mainstream media—from fashion spreads to sitcoms. Ever think that maybe the flat hand extended over the buttock is the new penis? At least there, our men can still exert some power.

Sad, though, isn't it? And not great for us, either. I mean, our behinds are getting sore. And aren't you tired of all these articles on our buttocks being the new breasts?

Let's refocus our men. Let's give them back their sticks.

Vive La Vulnerability

Here's how it's done. First, we created "roadblocks" to slow men down. Now we need to create "vulnerabilities" to keep men forging ahead despite these roadblocks. While a roadblock creates the much-needed tension and friction to arouse a man, he also needs to know that with effort, there is a path where resistance will finally be relinquished and he will succeed in his forward thrust.

We're not going to become Stepford Wives or porn stars without sexual needs of our own in order to make our men feel confident enough to press forward. And we're not going to start talking and acting as if we're twenty-three years old (unless you really are twenty-three, of course). But with a little understanding of the male psyche, we can help them build up their stick by showing a little vulnerability. We can get them to slow down, relax, and refocus on real women, because real women are not so scary, predatory, and demanding after all. Yes, real women are strong, proud, brilliant, independent, and powerful. But if a fella gets to know us, he will also realize that we actually have our weaknesses. And this makes us vulnerable.

The key to capturing a man's attention is to reveal our vulnerability in an artful and seductive manner. Artfulness is the key.

There are many kinds of vulnerabilities. Simply being "innocent" can be a vulnerability. For example, remember traveling to Italy and not knowing the language, but meeting that Italian architect? Even though he knew no English and you knew no Italian, the attraction was palpable. How was it that the time you spent together was so amazingly romantic? It's because without the orientation of place and language, you were reduced to being almost a child. The Italian architect was in control. And whether you consummated the affair or not there was undeniable erotic tension. And this made your man feel like a man.

This is why American men are so thrilled by foreign women. This is why they go for the dumb blondes, younger women, and the girl from a different culture, race, or religion. These girls step into the man's world (or at least this is how he perceives it) and he becomes the powerful one, the strong one, the all-knowing, all-seeing master of his universe.

Now, that's a big stick!

The Power of the Private Lane

I am not suggesting that you act dumb or younger than you are or that you fake a foreign accent or pretend you're from a different culture in order to make a man feel that he has a stick. But do consider how you can create vulnerability so that your roadblocks do not seem impossible to penetrate. Think of this vulnerability as being a private lane as opposed to an open road or a freeway.

Here's the difference between a roadblock and a private lane. A roadblock stops the man. You don't, however, want to completely stop him. You want to let him know that under the right circumstances, you might be amenable to more than a simple friendship. Still, you need a few No Trespassing signs to create a sense of exclusivity. This is different from a roadblock. It is certainly not the open road or a tollbooth. A private lane is for the woman who has discriminating tastes. She developed some kind of roadblock as the road narrows. It is difficult to enter a private lane, but not impossible. You may need a password. You probably have to know her friends and family. Sometimes, there's a big gate and a guard.

The purpose of creating a "private lane" then, is to seem—despite the roadblocks—approachable. Even vulnerable to entry. This is what's so appealing about private lanes. And I'm not talking about those wretched gated communities you'll find in Southern California where you're practically asked for a credit report and a urine sample before you may enter. I'm talking about those elegant private lanes you'll find along the shoreline in Westport, Connecticut. There's a little sign that says, "No Trespassing." Only residents or guests are permitted passage. The road narrows and sometimes there is a little booth, but generally no one is actually in the little booth, and well, you can drive down this road. But, it's risky business. They can spot an intruder from miles away. And the effect is more psychological that real. You tend to stay away if you don't belong. The key is a combination of approachability and exclusivity. So, throw in the roadblocks, yes, but also create a sense that you are indeed vulnerable to penetration. Does that sound like I'm talking about sex? Well, good. Because I am.

Here's a fact—men have a stick or a shtick. They have a penis. But this penis cannot and will not penetrate something that is completely boarded up. It needs to feel there is a potential for success. At the same time, the stick needs a certain amount of resistance to make it feel stimulated. A penis has very little interest in penetrating an eight-lane highway. There's no friction there. A penis wants to penetrate a tight little private lane.

Lifestyles of the Rich and Famous

Truly powerful women already know this. Just ask a very famous or wealthy woman and she will tell you she has developed strategies to make men feel not quite so intimated by her power. A woman with stratospheric status knows that she must give her man some kind of stick so that he can feel powerful enough to penetrate her—physically, psychically, emotionally. These powerful women will often cultivate vulnerabilities—perhaps an eccentricity or a pretty neurosis that makes them slightly childlike and seemingly vulnerable. Some vulnerabilities are rather unfortunate. For instance, they might make a fetish out of shabby chic furnishings. They might dress younger than their years, and become anorexic. Many dye their hair a shade of blonde that only young children possess. They begin to speak in a made-up accent and some will move to Nantucket and take to wearing childlike animal insignias on their clothing—ponies and black dogs and such.

But the concept of the vulnerability is still a good one, because it can be effectively used by all women to offset our power and create an air of penetrability, despite the fact that we also possess many roadblocks. So as you are developing your roadblocks, develop your vulnerabilities. Here are some archetypes. The key is to find out which one you feel most comfortable with and then modulate it for your own personality and needs. Subtlety and moderation is very important.

The Innocent

This vulnerability works well for young and old alike. While young women can authentically display a charming naïveté, older women who've been out of the dating scene can also create an air of innocence. You see the Innocent all around you—she often carries a cute little pocketbook and sometimes wears pigtails. She's partial to the Catholic Schoolgirl look, which, when done with subtlety, serves as a roadblock as well as a vulnerability.

The Rebel

If you like being naughty, occasionally drinking a little too much, wearing jeans, and breaking the rules, this one might appeal to you. It's especially effective with men who have a professor/disciplinarian stick.

The Virgin

Don't take this literally. The Virgin can be anyone who seems sexually repressed. You know, the buttoned-up librarian who wears thick glasses and her hair up in a bun that needs only a little coaxing before it comes tumbling down.

The Brain

This is a terrific vulnerability for women who think too much. Men love the challenge of bringing the Brain back to more earthy pleasures.

The Career Woman

She's related to the Brain. She also overworks and is out of touch with her sexuality. Many men find the challenge of reacquainting this type of gal with her sensual nature very thrilling.

The Androgyny Gal

She used to be called a tomboy. Her appeal is that in a way she's a virgin. She hasn't yet discovered what it means to a be real woman. Lots of men like to imagine they will awaken her to her female essence.

La Bohéme

She's the one with allergies, always coming down with a cold. She's a little childlike and may have an eating disorder. She appeals to men who like to rescue and protect.

The Starving Artist

No money. Broke. Artistic. This works especially well on men with a lot of money. But she doesn't care about money, only art! This obvious lack of common sense drives certain men to distraction.

The Not-So-Smart Girl

Just think Marilyn Monroe, Judy Holiday, Gracie Allen. They were smart, but they played up a certain kind of intellectual vulnerability that drove men crazy.

The Blonde

Blondes have more fun; the dumb blonde; the blonde bombshell. All myths. But men perceive it this way—she's dyed her hair blonde to send out a secret signal to men that she's hot!

The Foreigner

Just travel and you'll see how beautifully this one works. If you can't afford something overseas, just try going someplace where the accent is clearly different from your own. Get lost. Ask for directions. Your dance card will soon be filled.

The Older Woman

Aha! Good news for the *femme d'un certain âge*. In spite of what the media are constantly telling us, being an older woman can be very enticing. And it can be used as a roadblock *and* as a vulnerability. The next time a younger fella makes a pass, tell him, "Oh, I'm old enough to be your mother." He'll immediately tell you how old he is and how it's not true—you're just the right age for him. And older men like the Older Woman because they're excited by the prospect of reintroducing sex and reawakening her sexuality. Again, think the librarian type.

Now, once you've built up a man's stick through roadblocks and vulnerabilities, the question that arises is how to keep that stick feeling like a stick. How do you keep him coming back once he's satisfied? How do you make him wait for sex, then succumb with style, and get him back again? The key is to throw in constant roadblocks paired with vulnerabilities. In fact, smart gals create combination roadblock/vulnerabilities, so that sex never becomes easy or regular or routine. Sex should always surprising, challenging, and interesting. You are the bright blue fish in the stream, flashing against the light, then disappearing behind a rock. You are always a sport. Exciting. Difficult. Surprising. And yes, mesmerizing. A well-orchestrated roadblock/vulnerability will keep you from ever feeling taken for granted.

Romancing the Stick

After a time, you will also want to figure out what sort of stick your particular man is wielding. This is the key to building up the stick and keeping the stick at bay. Here is a selection of typical Male Sticks:

* Physical strength/prowess: "Oh, you're so strong. Can you open this jar of tomatoes?"
* Brains: "Oh, you're so smart. Can you explain quantum mechanics to me once again?"
* Money: "Oh, you're so rich. Could you pay for this book on the nature of the universe for me?"
* Talent: "I loved the way you sang that song. It was really brilliant! I wish I could sing like that!"
* Sex: "Wow, you sure know a lot of kinky positions. I don't know if I'm really ready to put that there. It seems kind of dangerous, dontcha think?"

Sometimes, men are not even aware that they are using their sticks and they can hurt us without consciously meaning to. But if we are aware that a man is trying to "penetrate" us (emotionally, then physically) with his stick, we can relax a little, and not get so upset. We can actually play with his stick. Let's go back to our Yale professor. Her date asked her how it felt to be so low on the totem pole. He was clearly using his stick in order to make her feel insignificant next to him. Rather than getting annoyed with this obvious ploy to pummel her, she could use this information (ah, he has a Career

Stick!) and then praise his work, so that he might stop metaphorically pushing her into the sand and trying to make her cry.

Why go to the trouble? Because if a man finds that one of his sticks isn't working, he'll keep poking around for vulnerabilities until he hits a nerve. Recently, a friend of mine told me of her male friend/paramour. This gentleman often tried to impress her with his career accomplishments, but my friend was completely unimpressed. Then, the other day, he called her up to tell her how he's busy interviewing interns and how he wished that fellatio was part of the job description (ha, ha, ha, very funny—not!). This kind of provocation was actually quite out of character for the fella. The joke fell flat for my friend and she became annoyed and upset. This man had found her vulnerability. But wouldn't it have been better if she had just allowed him to wave around his Career Stick in the first place so that he didn't have to sink to such low tactics as the "Aren't you going to get jealous now?" stick.

This is why we must teach our men that certain sticks will get them nowhere. We can do this by giving them Career Sticks, Strength Sticks, Intellectual Sticks, and Sex Sticks. Just watch out for those Psycho-Game Sticks and diffuse them quickly by not reacting. Psycho-Game Sticks include trying to make us jealous, criticizing our looks, our weight, how we budget our money, or ever comparing us with the Victoria's Secret models. (Unless he says we look just like one.)

While you may seem to have been conquered by the stick, you should always remain spiritually, if not literally, independent. This independence will constantly reawaken your man's stick because he will soon realize that although he metaphorically bopped you on the head with his big stick, he has not actually conquered you. Therefore, he must return again and again. This is how Stick Shift Theory works. Let him think he's zooming down the private lane in fourth gear, but then throw some speed bumps in the way to get him to downshift into first and work a little harder, concentrate a little more.

This way, the man keeps coming back. He feels there is some unfinished business. You are obviously not completely in awe of his stick. He has not completely conquered you. This is why you must have a coterie, flirt with everyone, and resist before artfully succumbing.

Consider all of those Katherine Hepburn-Spencer Tracy movies. Here's where you'll see the archetypal male fantasy. In *Woman of the Year,* our hero feels his male authority is being compromised by his lawyer-wife. So, Tracy confronts this strong/edgy/cranky/difficult/repressed woman and attempts to "break" Hepburn by using his force/intellectual power/psychological power/sexual power. By the film's end, our heroine has been made soft, malleable, vulnerable, and receptive. This is an extreme example, and of course we don't want this kind of power play and drama in our lives. But we do want the stick. When a woman gets into a fight with a fella and wins, she may think, "Oh, I really intimidated him!" Yes, she may have won the battle, but she has lost the war, because once the illusion of the powerful stick is swept away, the sex is ruined. A man needs his stick, and if it means backing down from an argument or flattering a fella—well, isn't that a small price to pay to ensure great sex?

What's so great about a man's stick? Why should we cater to his stick?

Very simply this—he has a stick and you don't. This is what makes things exciting. He has a penis! You have vagina. News flash: men and women are different!

Strangers in the Night

So, why not use this information to get the love you deserve? How? Play up your differences, your mystery, your inscrutability, your strangeness. Keep your man on his toes by being unpredictable, typically female (whatever that means to you—but make sure it means being different from your man). This is so that even after you've been together for years and years, he can never feel he has completely contained or conquered you. Men think we are a little flighty, given to excesses. Men think we are moody, chatterboxes, and spendthrifts. Men think we are capable of being easily distracted by shiny objects. Men think we are impressionable and easily seduced.

Now, our feminist nature balks at all of this. But consider for a moment the benefits we can derive from these male assumptions. Smart feminists don't waste their time trying to convince men out of their silly prejudices. Smart feminists artfully play with these assumptions to get what they want—in and out of the bedroom. Yes. Whether they own up to it or not, high-powered professional women use these tricks when it serves their purpose.

So, in addition to honoring your man's stick, reinforce your differences. Maintain your separateness, even if it's only in a psychic sense. Keep some secrets. No matter how long you've been with a man, remain individuated.

Love is overwhelming. Love is life-changing. Love keeps us from getting our work done. Lovers forget to eat, drink, get out of bed. Lovers don't return phone calls. Lovers swallow poison and die in each others arms.

So much rapture! No wonder we want to make fun of it. No wonder we want to dilute its power by separating sex from love. No wonder we pornographize love. No wonder we strive to take all the mystery out of it.

But don't you buy it! Put the mystery back in love. Forget about honest communication and open dialogue. All you have to do is praise the stick. Build a roadblock on a private lane and your man will come.

Ah, rapture.

chapter ten

Merge, Yield, and Proceed with caution

*How to avoid collisions
on the Internet*

The male gaze is powerful and controlling, and this is why men love the Internet. Here's a little history. Long before dating services became the fashion, many men were sitting in their boxer shorts in darkened living rooms all across America downloading porn. This was their first introduction to women and the Internet. The anonymity, the lack of consequence, the fantasy, the porn star—all this made the information highway go vroom-vroom! Men tend to be less social than women, embarrassed about their overwhelming sex drives, and shy when it comes to communicating with real women. So, the computer is a delicious resource for them. They can look at all the pretty pictures, get very interested and excited by one particular fantasy girl—say the one with the long blonde hair, the enormous silicone breasts, the rounded buttocks, the pouty, open-mouthed, anticipatory stare. After some time of contemplating this confection, he will bring himself to a froth and then quickly grow weary. He will look at his busty friend and suddenly feel a sense of incredible relief that well, she is not real. She is a fantasy. She will not start demanding things. She will not decide that this is a great time to talk about her problems paying the rent or how her sister-in-law just got a promotion and she didn't. Or how she really thinks the two of you need to spend more time together and maybe you could go to that craft fair in town on Saturday. Eeeeeks! What an incredible relief for the man to just turn the damn computer off and go to bed, knowing he has no responsibility for this gal. She is not real. She is just a porn star and this is her job.

On some level, we're aware that this is what's going on. But still, we cannot understand—why is it that during an era of such sexual freedom and promiscuity and oh-well-anything-goes, are men hiding out in their darkened homes, hunched over a computer screen? Why aren't they out there in the world, getting some? You may be asking yourself, how can real men prefer fake women over real sexually alive, ready-and-willing women?

I'll tell you why.

Real women scare the hell out of them!

Unfortunately, we haven't grasped this concept yet, and instead many women have decided that the only thing to do to get men's attention is to compete with the porn star. And so we've been dressing and acting the part.

Admit it. Aren't you sick of ridiculously low slung hip huggers and bare bellies? Aren't you getting bored with all the exposed breasts and buttocks? Don't you feel an overwhelming sense of desperate ennui every time you pick up a magazine and come face to face with Paris Hilton?

Pardon Me While I Rant

How did it happen that all the shadowy secret spider holes that were kept in the sole dominion of Internet pornography sites went so damned mainstream? Next thing you know, we'll see a Gap ad in the middle of your favorite *School Girls Get a Spanking* video. This is what happens when our culture gets usurped by big business. We see it all around us—this co-opting of our secret desires, our fears, and our wishes and private fantasies. And we are growing tired of it.

We are tired of the pornography of overabundant shopping malls, with their shiny new products thrusting and spilling their contents into our faces like some capitalist's wet dream.

We are tired of obscene SUVs hogging the road and taking up two parking spaces, because well, I'm just so large I can't fit into one of those tiny little parking spaces. I need two for my enormous off-roader, baby!

We are tired of coffee shops that serve only three different sizes of Large, Larger, and Extremely Large. Oh, and expensive, because well, I can afford it, toots.

And we are tired of our culture and art being turned into all-you-can-eat buffets and fast-food troughs.

And if we see another MTV video featuring hooker couture well, we might just explode.

The point is, we're living in a fast-food culture and the powers that be have handily usurped our sexuality (male and female, gay, straight, and bi, by the way) and used it to sell more stuff. More stuff to men (beer, cars, bikes, headphones, gadgets, computers, CDs, shaving cream, ratchets, and DVD players) and more stuff to women (cellulite cream, surgery, teeth whiteners, clothing, clothing, more clothing, shoes, lingerie, hair products, subzero refrigerators, cars, and cosmopolitans).

We are doing everything to keep up. We are donning the thongs, whitening the teeth, and wearing the Miracle Bras. (By the way, isn't this just a reinvention of the old padded bra?) Some of us are even getting surgery and dressing as if we are a piece of choice meat in the deli case. Look at this lovely loin. Oh, and we have a terrific rump roast here. How about these breasts. So tender!

Basically, we've been turned into porn stars.

No Virginia, You Are Not a Porn Star

But here's the deal. This hasn't brought men any closer to us. In fact, it really is scaring them off. The nice guys anyway. The guys who want a porn star will always be around—late at night, lurking in alleyways—only to disappear in the morning's light.

The truth is, most men don't really want to wake up to the light of day to have cornflakes and morning chitchat with a porn star. Men don't want to ask the porn star if she read that article in the *New York Times* about the endangered manatees. A guy doesn't want to look at the porn star in the light of day—among the clean white sheets and the photographs of his dog, Buddy, and the family on the Cape last summer. Porn stars are supposed to disappear in a cloud of smoke in the a.m. Poof! Like that. Because my God, think of the germs!

But there are no germs in the dark. There are no Cornflakes or family or faithful dog when a guy's with the porn star. That's because the porn star is not real. The porn star is a fantasy. And men like it that way. They'd like to occasionally get away from reality and have a fantasy or two. Don't you want to do this occasionally?

But we're spoiling the fantasy if we act like a porn star too. We're making it real. And we're automatically upping the porn ante. Yes. Consider the plight of the poor porn star. Now she's got all these ordinary women competing with her—acting like whores, running around in low-cut jeans with their thongs hanging out around their buttocks, talking about whips and chains at the PTA meeting and giant dildos as if they were on special this week at the Piggly Wiggly.

And you know why men go for the "girl next door"? Because she's not scary! The truth is, when it comes to sex, men have a lot to be afraid of, such as:

* Is his penis big enough?
* Is his penis as big as your ex-boyfriend's penis?

* What will you tell your girlfriends about him?
* Is his penis as big as the guy's penis in the porn video?
* Will you accuse him of date rape the next day?
* Is there any way to safely increase the size of his penis?
* Suppose he can't hmm…you know…uhh…get it up?
* What about those penis pumps? Do they really work?

You see the pattern here. It's all about the size and stamina of his penis. A guy can't keep this information under wraps once he's slept with you. This makes you very intimidating. Women don't worry about the size of their uterus. We don't worry about how erect we can become or quickly un-become. We can fake orgasm. (And yes, lots of men these days say they are faking orgasms too—sad, isn't it?) On top of all of this, men worry that we'll call all our girlfriends the next day and report the gory details. Oh and there's always the possibility that we can change our minds and call our lawyer!

Okay, I know none of you ever even think about doing any of these things, because you're all so good. But men certainly think about these things.

And this scares the hell out of them. This is why a lot of really nice guys have simply stepped away from the dating scene. This is why a lot of gals who feel invisible next to the porn stars have stepped away too. This is why many men have come up with whole new strategies that keep women from getting too close to them. Here are some techniques guys use to keep us at bay:

The Rules (For Men)

* Only sleep with women who come on strong, so there's a built-in disclaimer. "Hey, you were the one who seduced me, babe!"
* Only sleep with women you've just met, and then get out quick. "Good thing she never met any of my friends or family."

* Only have sex when out of town. "My name's Bob. That's right. Bob. Bob what? Bob. Just Bob. What are you, a detective?"
* Only have sex with toys or rubber dolls. "Gee, you're awfully quiet, honey. I like that in a woman."
* Only have sex with girls you meet on the Internet. "Hey, you're the one who put up your profile, babe!"

Yes, unfortunately, the Internet is really a boon for guys who are snakes. First off, all the work of meeting, chatting, flirting, and getting to know a woman has been done for them. Her profile is up. They know she wants to meet a man. They know what she's looking for and what buttons to press. After a couple of email exchanges, they meet for coffee. Not much of a monetary investment. And vroooom. They are on the super highway, having bypassed any kind of roadblock, intersection, detour, or spectator slow-down. Recently, a good friend of mine told me how she met a fella from Nerve.com. They went out, had a couple of drinks. By the end of the evening she was a little tipsy (read: roadblock/vulnerability) and "in love." And seemingly, he was too. As they were saying goodbye, he moved in close to her and said, "You want to kiss me, don't you?" My friend is highly evolved. Intelligent. Bright. Worldly. Honest. She kissed him lightly on the lips. It was a sweet gesture. Fun, flirtatious, and spontaneous. And, she reports, it was a great kiss. The next day, the man in question sends her a flirty email. So, she sends a flirty email back to him. The day after that, he sends my friend an email, saying "something has happened." Apparently, he got back together with his ex-girlfriend and he couldn't go out on any more dates. And that was the end of that.

Except, no. That was not it, because just a couple months later, she sees this guy is back on the Internet, trawling on Nerve.com. I guess he broke up with his girlfriend again. Perhaps he breaks up with his girlfriend often. Perhaps he breaks up with his girlfriend whenever he wants to have a little extracurricular activity. Perhaps he is simply using Internet dating services to boost his ego a bit. He's in a committed relationship, but he wants to know that if circumstances allowed, he could sleep with another woman. He wants to be assured that he is still desirable. He's not sleeping with any of these gals he meets through dating services. He is not initiating the first kiss. He is asking them if they would like to kiss him.

Is this so awful?

Trawling on the Internet

Let's say you're in a relationship and things become a little routine. Your boyfriend's attentions seem to be drifting and your attention is definitely drifting. You wonder, "Why doesn't he notice that I cut my hair and dyed it green? Is he going blind?" And so you might find yourself looking around and flirting with other fellas who do take notice of you and all your infinite variety of haircuts and colors, of mood changes and clothes and new shoes.

There's nothing wrong with this. And suppose a guy responds to you? He asks you out for coffee, all under the guise of a platonic friendship. He's really attentive and funny and sweet. He's practically courting you and you feel great. What's wrong with that? Nothing really. As long as you're not doing anything sexual and you keep it on a friendship level, there is nothing wrong with this. In fact, there are lots of things right about it. You feel happy, desirable. You've got a new member for your coterie. You light up. And you might bring this sense of desirability home to your lover/husband.

But, if you go onto an Internet dating service, there is something wrong with this. It's lying. It's lying to the partner/girlfriend/wife. And it's lying to the prospective Internet date. It's saying, "I'm single. I'm available. I'm looking for a date."

But this is what men often do on the Internet. They're already involved with a woman. Sometimes, they're actually married. But they want to know that they could have another woman, if they really wanted to enough. This is why the man my friend met asked, "You want to kiss me, don't you?" It's actually really telling. He didn't so much want to kiss her as he wanted to know she wanted to kiss him. Now, you might say—bastard, if he had a girl-friend, he should have made this clear up front! But the truth is, maybe he didn't have a girlfriend. Maybe he was just doing some comparison shopping. And maybe he just wanted to feel wanted. But maybe he thought, "Why get into something as complicated as a real relationship? Why not just go click, click, click and get yourself a date on Saturday night?"

It's so easy. And this is why the Internet is such a dangerous place. This is why you must proceed with extreme caution. Let's say you're an honest and straightforward gal. You put your pretty picture up, and your profile—about how you like walks in the sunset and your favorite book is *Love in the Time of Cholera.* Now, millions of guys are viewing you. Nice guys and not-so-nice guys. It's like you're standing on the side of an eight-lane superhighway with your thumb out, asking for a ride, holding a big sign that says, "I want a man!" Think about it. You're bound to meet some creeps. Everyone out there feels they have a right to contact you—eighty-year-olds (who look forty-ish—honest!), guys who put up photos of themselves bare-chested, guys who pose in their photos with their girlfriends ("Ready for a threesome, babe?"), men who can't figure out how to get a subject and verb to agree ("I'm looking for woman who like sunsets"), and guys who appear in their photos wearing big purple hats with feathers because they simply adore Merlin and all things magical!

Honey, you can't make this stuff up.

Maybe All They Need Is a Good Spanking

Oh, and here's another one. Recently, a new trend has emerged where guys in their twenties, fresh out of the womb of home and college, sign up on these dating services. But here's the catch—they don't actually want to date anyone their own age. Here's what they do. They look for women in their thirties and forties and then ask them if they can be their slave boys. Really. These young guys want to come over your apartment and clean it while you walk around in a black slip and stilettos and yell at them for being bad. "Very, very bad! And naughty! And bad!"

I guess they miss their mom.

But actually, it goes deeper than this.

They miss being put in their place. They miss being told they're naughty. They miss the sting of female disapproval. They miss knowing that there's such a thing as good and bad.

Now, does this mean we should all turn in our porn star outfits and change into our dominatrix get-ups?

No. No. No.

All right, so despite all these warnings, you still want to venture out on the Internet highway and you need to know how to do it without getting run over. First of all, get out a huge pile of roadblocks. Post a picture that's friendly, but not sexual. Same with your profile—be friendly, but not sexual. And be brief. Wait a long time to meet the guy. Talk to him a few times on the phone first. Make sure everything is kept absolutely friendly and nonsexual. This will discourage a good number of men and the ones who just want a quickie will go away. Good. When you do meet a man, make sure it's just for coffee, and again be friendly and nonsexual. If you're interested in him, then throw in the roadblock of your choice—either one you make up or one from chapter 8. This combination of being a nice, friendly gal who is simply not ready for romance will separate out the good seeds from the bad. If you really like a fella, add him to your coterie. Even if you really, really, really adore him, he must wait a long, long time. This is because you must erase from his brain any idea that you were seeking him out and that you needed him. He must believe he has not conquered you and therefore he must get his stick shift back into first gear and begin a fresh and inventive pursuit. This takes time. He must forget that he met you on the Internet. He must think of you as being so much more than a picture and a profile on a dating service. He must get to know you as a friend. The only way to do this is to overlay the first encounter with a history of shared experiences. Invite him to go out with your friends. Introduce him to your family. Show him that you are real. You are not a fantasy and not a porn star. Why go to all this trouble? Because men associate the Internet with fantasy sex and you need to do everything in your power to make him see you as real, someone of consequence.

So, yes, you can meet a guy through a dating service, but as soon as you decide you like him, pull him off the highway and onto a side road that's full of traffic— roadblocks and pretty complications.

chapter eleven

Fun with Freud

*How to keep his
motor purring*

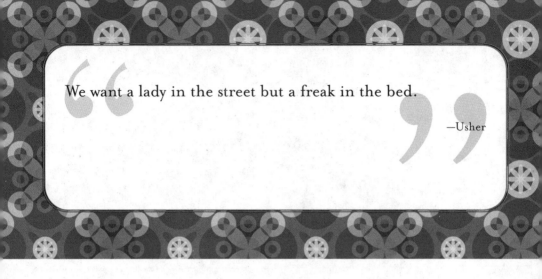

> We want a lady in the street but a freak in the bed.
>
> —Usher

Eroticism is a conduit. A magic tunnel leading into a million other dreams and memories, secret thoughts and desires. It is deep and limitless. Love is messy and complicated. Sex is part of the mess. And we need the mess. It's the fire in our bellies. It's so powerful, we need roadblocks and complications. We want to succumb, but we also want to resist. We want to be admired and loved and praised, but we also want to be punished and finally forgiven. We want to be longed for and obsessed over and we want to be left alone. We want heartfelt apologies and then we want many amends to be made. And we want to be reunited with our lover with sobs and laughter and whispered secret words that only we understand. And oh yeah, we want nothing short of reincarnation—to reemerge after a night of debauchery as the virgin bride, brand new in our lover's eyes. Innocent and girlish.

Gloria Steinem gave a speech a few years ago in New York City in which she described her newly married life. At some point in her talk, she addressed the women in the audience and suggested that we all try to discover the eroticism of equality.

In principle, it sounds very nice, doesn't it? Very tidy. But if you look at the words closely—eroticism of equality—well, it sounds like another one of those oxymorons like "casual sex." And doesn't the very idea of erotic equality sound extremely exhausting? And truthfully, terribly boring?

This is because eroticism has never been something one can put on a scale and measure. What we find erotic comes from the inequality of child/parent relationships, from domination, power, submission. Our sexual proclivities emerge and take shape out of our childhood fantasies, traumas, our teenage lessons, our grownup foibles. It comes from our secret encounters, our forbidden liaisons, the crimes we committed and the crimes that were committed against us. Into the mix, throw jealousy, revenge, God, religion, mother, father, your summer at Camp Mohawk, your horse, your seventh grade biology teacher, that famous movie star, the lost luggage, the trip to London, the kid in third grade with the big ears, the night you kissed Cynthia Beetlestein, the cool water in your next door neighbor's swimming pool, and the way it felt that early morning in August before anyone else was awake and you tiptoed out of your house in your nightgown, across the wet lawn to find the water a heartbreaking shade of turquoise blue.

Where does all this come from?

Childhood, mostly.

Words of Wisdom from the Esteemed Psycho-Therapist Adam Phillips

Think about it. Our first love object is our mother. We believe she is ours alone and then one day, we realize this is not true at all. In fact, she frequently goes off and sees this other person—this man! For a girl child, the response to this "infidelity" is to compete with the mother and try to wrest daddy's attention away from her. This is why we long for attention more than anything else. More than praise or love or punishment or pleasure. We want to be seen. We want to be seen as different from our mothers, but also similar. And often, this is how the world responds to us. Oh, what a pretty girl! Oh, look at your pretty dress! What lovely hair you have! And dimples too! You are so pretty! Pretty, pretty girl!

Boy children have a different experience. A boy quickly realizes that his mother's "infidelity" is with another male, like himself, but different. This other male is bigger and stronger and more powerful. This male does things. He comes and goes. He carries large objects and stomps around the house with a screwdriver and a ratchet. He doesn't sit around, dreamily letting the boy child suckle from his breast. No, he is up and about, full of activity and movement. And so the boy child competes with his father to wrest his mother's attention away from this bigger version of himself. He too, then becomes active, busy, banging blocks and constructing towers, throwing balls and marching around the house with a paper hat on his head, looking very official, declaring that he is the king of his kingdom. And so, he is praised for all his industry. And praised and praised.

So, ultimately this is want men want: to be praised for action.

And this is what women want: attention.

And yet, for all these differences, we have a great deal in common. We want both mother and father, safety and adventure, confinement and freedom, home and travel. This is how men experience Freud's mother/harlot complex. And we experience something I'll call the Rhett/Ashley Complex—that is, one man who is hard and strong and powerful and external (father), and another who is soft and safe and internal (mother). *Wuthering Heights* has Linton, who is connected to all things indoors—safety, warmth, civilized life—and Heathcliff, who roams the wild moors of Scotland, and is dangerous and unpredictable. You'll find this internal/external male paradigm all over popular fiction and film and if you examine your own heart, you will find that you want both, as well—the tough bloke on the motorcycle and the gentleman in the suit.

And how does this play out in our relationships? Well, we long for adventure and then we long to come home. We long to run away with a guy in the leather jacket on the Harley and then one day we suggest he ought to put on a suit and get a "real" job. We want a man who will be both mother and father to us. Both safe and dangerous. Often, we choose one, and then quickly grow dissatisfied and fantasize about the other. Eventually, hopefully, we find the two parts integrated in one man and we are happy. Oftentimes, we never do. (This, by the way, is why a coterie and light flirtations are essential throughout our life—because no one man will ever satisfy all our needs.)

The same goes for men, except they notice early on that they are different from their mothers. Their anatomy is different. This creates all sorts of additional complications. First of all, there is the fear that when a man is with a woman and she is too nice, too close, too comfortable—she will swoop him back into an infantile or even prebirth state. Scary stuff. After all, a child's first understanding of the vagina is that it is the place where babies come from, specifically where he came from. This idea is fixed in the child's mind long before the notion that the vagina is also a place to be entered by the male. For a boy child, who has no vagina, it's a place of mystery and wonder, but also a threatening place, always calling his name like a siren to, "come home, sailor."

This is why men are attracted to younger women, less powerful women, less maternal women. They never fully recover from the fact that a woman has such power over them. We know they worry about it. The insatiable female is universally feared, and so, we consciously or subconsciously strive to reassure our men that we are just girls, innocent, really, or that we are whores, not protective or nice, and we certainly will not be baking any chocolate chip cookies! The point is we strive to convince men that we are nothing like their mother at all.

Why, It's Little Red Riding Hood

And these days, when women are obviously gaining great strides in the corridors of power, it's not easy to pose as the powerless "girl" or outsider "harlot." So we offer men an additional reassurance that we are not really all that intimidating by going way out of our way to stay girlish and seemingly powerless (even while running a Fortune 500 company). We install plastic Barbie breasts onto our chests. We color out the first strand of gray in our hair and we wear childish clothes—whether it's the tomboy look or the bad schoolgirl or the high school tramp look. We refuse to dress like grownup women, unless we are young enough to do it with a huge dose of irony. In our quest for girlishness, we have even taken to waxing off our pubic hair as a way of saying, "See, I'm not even pubescent! I'm just a child! You have no fear that I'll swallow you up and take you back into the swampy bog of your original amorphous state!"

We do all of this to counterbalance our own increasing power in our professional and financial lives, because we know on some level we are scaring men off and our love lives are suffering.

And yet for all this, men do desire both the mother and the girl in their relationships. To be honest, men do like home cooking. And they do like having someone straighten up around the house. This rankles our feminist sensibilities—we know that they will flee the maternal as soon as they've downed the last cookie with the last glass of cold milk. And so many of us decide the only thing to do is never be maternal.

However, oftentimes, a man will install a motherly gal at home and then proceed to stray. The woman at home may be beautiful or not, brilliant or not—the point is she's reliable. She is non-threatening. She will always be there. And generally, she does cook and clean and buy the groceries, and drops his suit off at the dry cleaners. She's not the type to run off with the mailman or get involved with the barista at Starbucks. She's not bad in bed. She might be a good mother, too. This is a perfect situation for a man who wants Freud's paradigm of mother and harlot, because while men are shored up by the comforts of home, they are also suffocated by these comforts. And so our man finds himself a chippie elsewhere. She has many qualities, but generally she is not particularly maternal. She is often a younger woman, someone with less power. She is his harlot and mistress. His adventure and dangerous liaison. His little girl and protégé. She provides the friction and the seductive feeling that he is hurting "mommy"; he is being disobedient and disloyal and just plain bad. This makes him feel he is getting back at his own mommy for the betrayal of his little boy self, her taking up with daddy. But, more than this, the harlot/girl/mistress is the one he can run to when he feels that all his power is being sucked out at home and that he is in danger of being swallowed up by the maternal.

California Girls

And for those men who do not have a maternal type waiting at home with a hot bowl of soup, this harlot/mistress/little girl can serve as the roadblock that keeps a real woman from entering his life and drowning him. Recently, a friend of mine was set up on a date with a very wealthy, very handsome gentlemen from Southern California. He seemed like an appropriate match. They were both the same age, in their late forties, both professionals, both intelligent and accomplished. My friend and this gentleman were having a lovely time, and then over dinner, he proceeded to tell her all about his bisexual girlfriend in northern California. He told her how his bisexual girlfriend (twenty years his junior) was actually on a date with a woman that very night. Later, this man suggested that perhaps one day, they might indulge in a threesome. All this, on the first date!

But think what an interesting roadblock he has placed in the way of any woman who might want to get too close to him (or his money, perhaps). For the women in his hometown in Southern California, he has a bisexual lover/girlfriend to serve as a sort of unseen chaperone, throwing cold water into the works. And for the bisexual girlfriend—well, he keeps her at arm's length by insisting she not move from San Francisco to Southern California, even though she would very much like to. (And one does wonder—is her bisexuality her roadblock to keep him from running away?)

So you see, the fear of being swallowed up and infantilized by the "mother" is obviously very, very strong. And on some level, we understand consciously or unconsciously this male fear and so we try to vanquish our maternalism. Some of us grow hard and sleek and steely. We become strong, muscled, independent professional women, a bit hardened and a little brittle. Some of us will sugar coat our demands with little girl mannerisms—"Ooooh, Bobby, would you pleeeeasssse take the trash out for little old me?" Some of us dress like streetwalkers, or wear jeans and baseball caps to proclaim, "We're just one of the boys. Honest! Don't be afraid! Just move over while I hit a curve ball and steal second base."

Girls and Goats

We do all this in an effort to say, "No, we're not maternal. We're not like your mother!" Why? Because we know that as soon as we turn into the metaphorical mother, our partner will have to find an interloper to create a triangle. She represents the unfamiliar. And usually the interloper is child-like, not necessarily bright or accomplished. She is different. In fact, sometimes the interloper is a goat, just like in Edward Albee's excellent play *Who Is Sylvia?* or *The Goat*.

But still, inside of us there really is a vulnerability and softness. Inside, we have hidden this ache for *maternalism*. And so, when a man comes along, one that we really, really like and give our heart to, we want to relax.

Often, after all these struggles to stay girlish and thin and independent and strong, we fall in love with a man and we suddenly collapse into the cushiony glow and comfort of his love. We want to stay at home and never go out. We want to cuddle under the covers where it's safe and warm and have breakfast in bed—bagels and lox and coffee with real cream. We want to cook huge pots of hearty stews and hang some lace curtains.

You see, it's the same principle found in fasting and binging. We become all "girl," denying the existence of our maternalism until one day we get a little taste of being maternal and soft and we devour it like a woman who has deprived herself of chocolate for years. We can't stop. We can't pretend to be unavailable or busy or independent or a little cool. "My God, it's chocolate— I mean, it's a man in my bed and he's really, really nice! And I want more and more and more and more and gobble, gobble, gobble!"

And then one day we tell our man to stop splashing water around the sink, and suddenly our man announces that he is drowning in Laura Ashley sheets and screams he can't breathe and he runs for the door as we cling to his right calf, crying, "I need you!"

The Either/Or Complex

In the opposite extreme, there are women who are all "mother" and they've deprived themselves of the independent, adventurous "girl" within. These women tend to literally be mothers. They thrive on taking care of others. They like to bake bread. They seldom leave the house. They are constantly redecorating and making crafts for the holidays. They like to go to the mall because it's so interior and big and safe and warm—like one big, happy womb. Men actually quite adore these women. They remind them of their mothers. But, these very same men will find themselves a "girl" who will bring some yang to the yin—oh yeah, and some hot sex. And the maternal woman? One day, she'll wake up and say, "Hey, you're not a baby! You're a man! Act like one!" And he will scream back, "How come you never wear a bustier and g-string and prance around the house like a slut anymore?"

Celebrate Your Duality

You see the problem here—if we are all girl or all mother, we are creating an emotional imbalance. Knowing this, the answer to how to keep a man's motor purring is quite straightforward. We must strive for balance. We must embrace our own duality. Freud calls this duality the mother and the harlot. I am adding Heathcliff and Linton to show the duality as it applies to the female psyche, because I believe that both men and women experience this as an early consequence of realizing that their mother—their first love object—has been "unfaithful" to them with their father. Here are the qualities inherent in each archetype:

Heathcliff/Harlot	Linton/Mother
* Adventurous	* Safe
* Unpredictable	* Predictable
* Independent	* Dependent
* Out in the world	* At home
* Self-centered	* Centered on others
* Wild	* Protective
* Free	* Confined
* Yang energy	* Yin energy
* External	* Internal

So, as women, knowing this about our men, how could we integrate within ourselves the duality of harlot and mother—how could you be free and dependent? How could you be wild and protective? How could you be both unpredictable and centered on others?

Still, there is an important function inherent in the division of mother and harlot. For a man, this division creates a triangle in which he is the center between two women. One of these women is the "mother." As a parental figure, she creates an obstacle, a roadblock that keeps the man from completely straying too far with the harlot(s). The late psychoanalyst Stephen A. Mitchell calls this phenomenon the "Beast on a Leash," wherein a male might construct a situation in which he is a "wild, dangerous, pansexual creature who, if not for her control over him, would be ravishing every woman in the neighborhood."

We, too, create triangles. Often, we will find ourselves a paternal male, install him as our steady, reliable boyfriend, and then keep an eye open for the wild Heathcliff male to enter into the paradigm. Some of us like to fantasize about two men fighting over us, competing for our attentions, just as we might wish our mother and father had paid attention to us, rather than to themselves. The nerve of them.

Ultimately, both men and women set up triangles. Both of us need the roadblock/obstacle/parental figure to add friction, tension, and an authority figure that allows us to play the naughty child and pursue our object of desire with the sense of drama that only the forbidden can bring to the fore. One plays anima, the other animus.

Lucy/Ricky Theory

If you can recall the old *I Love Lucy* sitcom, you'll see what I mean—although just about every sitcom today has its version of the Lucy and the Ricky. Lucy is a bundle of contradictions. She is a devoted wife and mother and yet she is always striving. She is always getting into trouble, but she is always forgiven. She is childlike and yet she is clever and very ambitious and occasionally entrepreneurial. She is the star of the sitcom, but not the star in Ricky's nightclub act. In fact, she has to fight and trick him to get on it. Nonetheless, it is her show. She is the trouble-maker, the shapeshifter character, the perennial child, and the one that keeps the more parental fig-ure, Ricky, on his toes. She does this by alternating between being wildly uncontrollable and prettily (okay, sometimes not-so-prettily) contrite. But more than this, Lucy and Ricky have Fred and Ethel—older upstairs neigh-bors who provide yet more obstacles, roadblocks, and parental figures.

Ricky loves Lucy because she is full of dualities. She embodies both the mother and the harlot. Ricky is never in danger of being suffocated by her female nature, because she is constantly in movement, switching from girl to grownup in a flash. She is both Hillary Clinton and Monica Lewinsky, all rolled into one woman.

On some level, we know that men thrive on staging a triangle, where two women (the harlot and the mother) are fighting over them. Much of litera-ture and film centers around this power struggle. Sometimes we play the pro-fessor and sometimes we play the student. Sometimes we are mommy and sometimes we are bad little girl. Sometimes he plays the boss and we play the assistant. Sometimes he's the Republican and we are the Democrat. Sometimes he is England and we are Northern Ireland.

Boredom sets in when we refuse to embrace our own duality. We are at all times both mother and harlot. The key is not to tell our man this obvious fact, but to show him.

How to Stage a Spat

One way is to stage a spat. But be sure to have some fun doing it. Choose a side: harlot or mother and then (the next time you feel your man's attention drifting) say something a little provocative. Oh, and wear a great outfit. If you're playing harlot, get out your bustier. If it's mother you're playing, try a vintage 1940s housedress.

Next, consider your man's stick. His stick will determine how you want to be provocative. For example, if he's the finance expert in the house, try buying something expensive and then tearfully "confess to the crime."

There's a beautiful demonstration of this technique in Cynthia Kling's essay, "Staying Bad, Staying Married." In it, she describes how she bought a ridiculously expensive cashmere sweater and how her friend told her husband about the purchase. A battle ensued over the sweater in which he tried to coerce her into returning it, but she dug in her heels and stubbornly refused. The sweater conflict raged for days, the tension building. They could think of little else, they forgot to eat or sleep or take the dog for a walk. Okay, I made that last part up. The point is, Cynthia finally returned the sweater, which she confessed she didn't really even like all that much. But you see, by letting her husband "win" a victory, and by letting him "feel like a whacked-out South American dictator," she has instilled much spice into their marital relationship. And I bet they had a lot of hot sex afterward.

Think about it—a sweater is of little consequence. If we allow our men to occasionally get out their big stick and shake it at a cashmere sweater, we keep the fires burning, we honor the stick, and we keep our relationship from going flat. Her husband was suddenly the big daddy who had to punish his naughty, spendthrift wife. "Oh, dear!"

Trivial Pursuits

The key to staging a fun spat and letting a little role-playing enter your relationship is to choose something fairly inconsequential that you are willing to fight over and then give in to, such as a sweater. And by the way, you can also accuse your partner of some infraction and punish him. It's only fair, after all. The key is to stay away from truly sensitive areas in your relationship, but why not accuse your partner of being insensitive to—you fill in the blank. ("You tyrant! How dare you accuse me of always losing my keys! By the way, have you seen my keys?")

And you can also take a Stick Shift moment and put it in reverse. For instance, a good friend of mine told me how her husband recently caught her by surprise in the upstairs hallway. He picked her up and whirled her around. But in doing so, he bumped her elbow against a wall. She said it hurt, and he grabbed his stick (a stupid one, at that) and said, "Well, if you weren't so heavy, it wouldn't have happened." Now my friend is anything but heavy. In fact, she is quite svelte. And so she used the opportunity to fret over his cruelty and to stage a spat. Finally, he begged for her forgiveness and they had lovely sex to celebrate their making up.

Now, many of you will say that this is dishonest! This is manipulative! This is playing a game!

Yeah, and so what? Don't you want to have some fun? Don't you want to spice up your love life? Don't you want to keep your man from running off with Monica Lewinsky? Don't you want to keep all that harlot/mother obsession at home with you? The answer is to embrace your duality.

Besides, accusing women of being manipulative and playing games is just another way to marginalize us, devalue our female nature, and get us to act more like men. It is in the male interest to separate us from ourselves. It is to their benefit to have all the harlots on one side of town and all the well-behaved mommies on the other side of town. But this is just another form of bondage, and I am telling you now that by embracing your own duality you will get men to sit up, take notice, and pay attention, (before you change your mind again).

We will never be predictable. We will never be simply one thing or the other. We will embrace our sexual selves, our changing, wild, home-bound, free, crazy, rational, self-centered, sacrificing selves.

B.F. Skinner's Guide to Driving Men Crazy

Consider B. F. Skinner's research on human behavior. He built on Pavlov's findings of stimulus and response. You know, the guy who rang a bell and gave out treats. After a while, he didn't even need to use the treats, because the bell was enough to elicit the same response. Skinner found that there are three kinds of behaviors in human relationships. The first is the person who is nice, nice, nice, nice. The second is the type of person who is mean, mean, mean, mean. And the third is the person who is the one who is nice, nice, nice, *mean*! Then nice, nice, nice again before doing something very naughty. As it turns out, Skinner found that most people fall in love with the third personality type—the inconsistent person. Why? Because we generally feel more alive in the presence of someone who is volatile, who may reward us, but then again, may just punish us.

This is the secret to a man's heart. Punish him! No, I'm just kidding. Here's what we need to do: first, be nice, nice, nice. Be sweet, cheerful, understanding, and kind. Behave yourself, don't drink too much, dress like a lady, be polite and proper and intelligent. Cook him a nice dinner, laugh at his jokes, flatter him, and after a while, sleep with him. Then every once in a while—bite him. Be bad, difficult, contrary, and very, very naughty!

This is not as easy as it sounds. And the style of your naughtiness must be specific to your relationship and suit your personality, your built-in roadblocks, and your man's stick or shtick. Basically, how you stage your spat, how you misbehave, is determined by all those messy things that go into creating your own individualized roadmap to Eros. Consider your childhood traumas, your teenage foibles, your secret desires, your partner's basic needs and vivid memories. All this goes into the mix. Oh, yes, and your own duality. Embrace it and balance the harlot with the mother, the bad girl with the good woman.

Gloria Steinem Had a Point

So, perhaps, after all, Gloria Steinem had it right when she suggested we find the equality in eroticism. Only, the equality is not between a man and a woman, but the equality we need to find is between the two halves of our own female selves.

PART FOUR

How to Start a Revolution

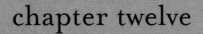

chapter twelve

Take Back the Sex Month

Time to boycott!
Mark your calendars

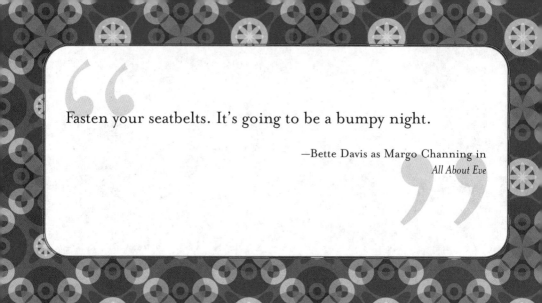

> Fasten your seatbelts. It's going to be a bumpy night.
>
> —Bette Davis as Margo Channing in
> *All About Eve*

Men are in the catbird seat. And they know it. In the meantime, we're still bending over backward to please them. We sleep with them on the third date. We give up all our male friendships for them. We wait by the phone for them to call. Or we call them at the appointed time they've told us to call them. We wear the outfits they like, the heels, the push-up bras, and we lose a whole lot of sleep worrying about what they think about and why they haven't called us back and when we ask why, we're told "he's just not that into you."

Well, I'll tell you what he is into. Sex!

It's really that simple. Men want sex and praise. We want sex and attention. But, because we've created such a plethora of sexual opportunities and an endless visual feast—an all-you-can-eat buffet of twenty-four-hour available sex—we've got a megastore situation on our hands.

This is how men think. Why should they put in all the effort and time on some gal who makes him wait and takes her time before granting him her sexual favors? Why not just go for the chippie who'll hit the sack after a bad come-on line and a couple of brewskies?

If we go along with this, we too are supporting the megastore mentality of sex.

And, unfortunately, if we're not succumbing so easily, and not supporting the megastore mentality of sex, we end up sitting by the sidelines, wondering why we have no dates and there's a big going-out-of-business sign in our date book. This is what's happened to romance. It's been completely devalued and undersold because of cheap sex from gals who haven't been politicized.

Get Political

So, what are we going to do? Because the truth is, we can individually try to start a revolution—we can make him wait for sex, we can flirt freely, we can build a coterie and develop tantalizing roadblocks—but if there are all these other gals out there who will simply supply and succumb (often without style, by the way) well, then we have an uphill battle on our hands.

The answer is to unionize! Educate our sisters! Boycott! Strike! Women of the world unite! No more megastores of sex! No more fast-food dating! Destroy the male monopoly! Take back the sex!

Yes, the revolution starts here. If we don't join together as a united front and take back the sex, nothing is going to change. Together, we can change the world.

How are we going to do this? First, let's admit that the current dating paradigm is not working for any of us.

Consider the ancient Greek comedy by Aristophanes, *Lysistrata.* In this wonderful play, Lysistrata convinces all the women to refuse to have sex with their lovers or husbands until they put down arms and end the war between Athens and Sparta. And you know what? Her plan worked. So here's what I'm suggesting.

The Boycott Begins

Mark your calendars for the month of August. Why August? Because that's the month when psychiatrists, psychoanalysts, and psychotherapists traditionally go on vacation, and besides, August is generally hot and sticky.

This August will be hotter and stickier than ever.

If it's sex that drives men, that makes men work and plan and strategize and even take seminars on how to succeed with women—then let's take back the sex. Let's stop the feeding frenzy and put our men on a diet. No more fast-food sex. They're completely satiated anyway, so addicted to the easy in and easy out that they've forgotten what good sex is really like. And they certainly have lost the art of courtship and abiding love. Here's what happened. Somewhere in their primal DNA men learned to hunt for their food, and because food was not always available their bodies developed the ability to store fat to keep them alive during periods of famine. But modern man, living in an era of overabundance and availability of limitless food options, has grown fat.

Well, it's the same with sex. The hunting instinct is still there, but it's dormant because we offer a plethora of sexual opportunities (real and imagined) and men have just gotten lazy. We've given our hunters an enormous overflowing discount supermarket of sex. It's open twenty-four hours a day. There are everyday low prices and hundreds of bargains. An excellent return policy—no questions asked. It has hundreds of varieties and flavors and sizes and shapes. It's instant! Oh, and it's chock full of artificial ingredients. Welcome to the megastore of sex!

Oy vey!

All right, so it happened. Now what can we do about it? How can we shut down the doors to this monstrosity of modern living? How can we get men to reconnect with their primal instincts and get off their fat behinds and truly work at capturing our hearts? How can we sound the alarm?

Unionize!

If we as women work together on this, we can truly wake up these cads and turn the world of courtship around. Consider all the willpower we women put forth in our efforts to lose weight. Consider our workout regimens, our diets, our carefully orchestrated plans for self-improvement. Now, let's use this strength, this genius, this creativity and willpower to get men back into line. For too long, we've let men treat love as a drag race—all over and done with in five minutes. Let's bring back the ideals of the marathon sports car competition, *Le Mans Endurance*. It's not just about strength and skill, it's about endurance. That's the kind of man you want—a man with endurance. A sleek, strong, pre-fast-food man who is directed and focused and willing to put down the channel changer, get up off the couch, take you in his arms, and work at capturing your heart again and again and again.

Let's bring back romance. Honestly, for the last thirty-five years romance has been thrown out the window for pure, unadulterated sex. And yes, sex is good, but without some degree of romance, passion, adventure, and struggle, sex is dull. We're on overload right now. What's forbidden? What's kinky? What's secretive? What's dirty? What's really taboo? Not much. And this is because popular culture has capitalized on female sexual mystery, turning the most forbidden fantasies into fodder for late-night cable TV shows. This is another way to degrade and devalue our sex and create an atmosphere of seeming over-abundance. It's the megastore mentality again. Flood the market. Slash prices. It's another ploy to make women believe that their sex is worth little because obviously every other gal in the country is exposing her breasts on *Girls Gone Wild* and maneuvering herself into a sexual liaison with a creep in *Elimidate* or competing for Flavor Flav's attention, where in reality, none of this is happening! It's just male wishful thinking. But it grinds away at the subconscious mind, and viewers—both male and female—begin to believe it's true. In the meantime, our senses grow dull and sated and the power of our sex is slowly being diminished through over-exposure.

But, you know what—and here's the good news—it'll never really completely happen. Our sex will always be mysterious and magical, threatening and captivating, mesmerizing and awe-inspiring. No matter how they try to trivialize it.

Take Back the Sex!

Let's put the sex back in sex. Let's rediscover our shadow sides, our shape shifters, the secret dark corners of our sexual psyches.

Let's bring back the art of flirting without fornicating. Let's insist on being truly pursued, wooed, and courted. Imagine this—a world where men and women meet in groups and alone, go to parties and concerts and cafes, and flirt, a lot. These flirtations carry no weight, no promise of anything more. They are simply for fun and delight. Friendships are formed. Crushes are created. And then, yes, once in a while, this flirtation develops into something deeper, but not for quite a while. As women, don't we deserve a little time and space (just as we take longer in bed, and want more), shouldn't we demand this in our romance? The women's magazines give us advice on how to make our men slow down so that we get our pleasure. So why not do the same before we get into bed—can't we slow things down there? The truth is, we make so few demands. We want romance. And by the way, romance is not about a man spending a lot of money. It's about taking time, it's about manners, kindness, attention, focus, and true courtship.

Let's think globally. If we all pull together, then the men of the world will sit up and take notice and change their ways. We must unite for this cause. All of us. If you're a twenty-something, it may seem easy and fun and cool to have a quickie with the clerk at Urban Outfitters. After all, the idea of marriage may be a long way away for you, and you want to experiment and learn about life and have fun and experience everything. But the truth is, if you're busy sleeping with a bunch of guys and not getting serious with any of them, you'll be too distracted to notice when your *bashaert*, your true soul mate, comes along. You know, that guy you'd like to spend your whole life with. Also, if you live in a small town or you move in one particular group, word gets around.

Dump the cads!

And, if you're twenty-five and sleeping with a forty-something fella, well, there's karma to consider. Many of these gentlemen are serious, but be wary of the cads. These are the guys who start out at nineteen and then play the field until they hit forty, when they discover that women their age wake up and say, "Hey, I'd like to get married and have kids someday." Many forty-year-old guys are in no hurry. Some of them imagine they'll play the field for another twenty-five years. Sometimes these older men use their money to prey on young women and pretend to be hipsters, but they are vampires stealing our youth. Oftentimes we wake up one day to find we are thirty-five and hankering for a baby and that's when the vampire makes his speedy yet mysterious exit. Knowing this, begin thinking early on about who your soul mate is, and please don't waste your time and youth on cads, bounders, scoundrels, or bon vivant aesthete men-about-town who are here today and gone tomorrow.

If we boycott these playboys and force them to become serious, this is going to create a whole new resource of available men for the over-thirty-five crowd. Men are going to have to start looking at women their own age for a change. Nonetheless, all of us have to take our sex seriously and stop playing the field, because if we're sleeping with whatever fella comes our way, then there's a very good chance we won't even notice our soul mate when he quietly enters our life. We'll be too busy bedding Bob and Joe and Mark and Tom and Fred. The problem with multiple dating is that we never really get to know the fella, we never learn how to really nurture a relationship and help it grow, and so it's easier to just get rid of one guy and get another. But one day, the well is going to dry up. It may happen when you're twenty-eight, thirty-seven, or forty-two. But one day, you will suddenly discover you're no longer the "It" girl. You will wake up one day and discover something terrible has happened—you've lost your sense of confidence, and you've started to feel old (and this can happen in your twenties).

But here's what you can do right now, whether you're twenty or seventy.

Unite!

Mark Your Calendars for August

Let's take our cue from *Lysistrata*. There will be no sex until men meet our demands. And if waiting a month for sex still sounds incredibly difficult then get yourself a good vibrator, take up horseback riding, learn how to knit, or go to Italy and have a secret international liaison.

And how will we spend August? Here's what I propose. Let's rally at our local singles bar/club/whatever. Let's wear great clothes, order drinks, and have a lot of fun, laughing and flirting. (Oh, and be sure to have a cock-block/designated driver.) No one goes home with a guy. Let's have girl get-togethers á la *Sex and the City*. How about pajama parties? Cosmopolitan night? Let's write our own mating manifesto and create a third wave of consciousness raising. Let's take back the sex. Let's frequent businesses that support romance and courtship. Let's throw sexual revolution parties. Let's form clubs. Let's start our own companies that promote romance and courtship and love. Yes, love! Vive la révolution!

Works Cited

Ackerman, Diane. *A Natural History of the Senses*. New York: Vintage Books, 1990.

Bakos, Susan Crain. *What Men Really Want*. New York: St. Martins Press, 1990.

Bentley, Toni. "Toni Bentley Defends Her Saucy Confessional." *New York Times*, 22 Nov. 2004.

Berkowitz, Elana. "Are You With Him? Why Yes, Want to Date Him?" *New York Times*, 10 Oct. 2004. Section 9.

Copeland, David and Ron Louis. *How to Succeed with Women*. New Jersey: Parker Publishing Company, 1998.

David, Anna. "Friends with Benefits." *Razor*, Oct. 2004.

Denizet-Lewis, Benoit. "Friends, Friends with Benefits and the Benefits of the Local Mall." *New York Times Magazine*, 30 May 2004.

Doane, Mary Ann. *The Desire to Desire*. Indiana: Indiana University Press, 1987.

Elder, Rachel. "What Up, Wimpster?" *Bust*, Summer 2004. 48–51.

Fein, Ellen and Sherrie Schneider. *The Rules*. New York: Warner Books Incorporated, 1995.

Flora, Carlin. "Chemistry Lessons: Making Love's First Blush Linger On." *Psychology Today*. Sept./Oct. 2004.

Freud, Sigmund. *Sexuality and the Psychology of Love*. Ed. Phillip Rieff. New York: Touchstone Books, 1997.

Gerstman, Bradley Esq., Christopher Pizzo, CPA, and Rich Seldes, MD. *What Men Want*. New York: Cliff Street Books, 1998.

Gettleman, Jeffrey. "Rape Case Stuns Parents, Engrosses Students." *New York Times* 10 Oct. 2004. 41N.

Gray, John PhD. *Men Are from Mars, Women Are from Venus*. New York: HarperCollins Publishers, 1992.

Green, Penelope. "Books of Style: An Exultation of a State of Mind: Bohemian Manifesto." *New York Times*, 24 Oct. 2004. ST12.

Hanauer, Cathi. Ed. *The Bitch in the House*. New York: Perennial, 2002.

Hirschberg, Lynn. "The Redeemer." *New York Times Magazine*, 5 Sept. 2004. 26.

Jacobs, Andrew. "Call Girls, Updated." *New York Times*, 12 Oct. 2004. B1.

John, Warren St. "In an Oversexed Age, More Guys Take the Pill." *New York Times*, 14 Dec. 2003. Section 9.

Jung, C. G. *Memories, Dreams, Reflections*. Trans. Richard and Clara Winston. New York: Vintage Books, 1965.

Kerner, Ian PhD. *She Comes First*. New York: Reagan Books, 2004.

Marin, Rick. *Cad: Confessions of a Toxic Bachelor*. New York: Hyperion, 2003.

Martin, Steve. *Shopgirl*. New York: Hyperion, 2000.

Mitchel, Stephen A. *Can Love Last?* New York: W. W. Norton & Company, 2002.

Moore, Doris Langley. *The Technique of the Love Affair*. Ed. Norrie Epstein. New York:

Pantheon Books, 1999.

Kipnis, Laura. *Against Love: A Polemic*. New York: Pantheon Books, 2003.

Paglia, Camille. Ed. *Sex, Art, and American Culture*. New York: Vintage Books, 1992.

Pollitt, Katha. "Learning to Drive." *New Yorker*, 22 July 2002. 36–40.

Roiphe, Katie. *Last Night in Paradise*. New York: Little, Brown & Company, 1997.

Shalit, Wendy. *A Return to Modesty*. New York: Touchstone, 1999.

Shulevitz, Judith. "Danger: Romantic Love." *New York Times* Book Review, 10 Feb. 2002. 27.

Sobel, Beth. "Girl Magnet." *New York Post*, 4 June 2004. 39–40.

Sohn, Amy. "The Enablers." *New York Post*, 22 Nov. 2004. 66.

Swift, Daniel. "What's Love Got to Do with It?" *New York Times* Book Review, 3 April 2005. 31.

Wolf, Naomi. *The Beauty Myth*. Toronto, Canada: Vintage Books, 1990.

Bibliography

Argov, Sherry. *Why Men Love Bitches*. Massachusetts: Adams Media Corporation, 2002.

Berkowitz, Bob and Gittines, Roger. *What Men Won't Tell You but Women Need to Know*. New York: Avon Books, 1990.

Breton, Andre. *Nadja*. Trans. Richard Howard. New York: Grove Press, 1960.

Clink, Tony. *The Layguide*. New York: Citadel Press, 2004.

Faldi, Susan. *Backlash*. New York: Anchor Books, 1992.

Foucault, Michel. *Madness and Civilization*. Trans. Richard Howard. New York: Vintage Books, 1973.

Friday, Nancy. *My Secret Garden*. New York: Pocket Books, 1973.

Friday, Nancy. *Our Looks, Our Lives*. New York: Harper Paperbacks, 1996.

Greene, Robert. *The Art of Seduction*. New York: Penguin Books, 2001.

Jong, Erica. *Fear of Fifty*. New York: Harper Perennial, 1997.

Phillips, Adam. *Monogamy*. Canada: Vintage Paperback, 1999.

Phillips, Adam. *On Flirtation*. Massachusetts: Harvard University Press, 1994.

Slater, Lauren. *Opening Skinner's Box: Great Psychological Experiments of The Twentieth Century*. New York: W. W. Norton & Company, 2005.

Sprengnether, Madelon. *Crying at the Movies*. Minnesota: Graywolf Press, 2002.

Steinberg, David. Ed. *The Erotic Impulse*. California: Jeremy P. Tarcher/Perigee, 1992.

Vogler, Christopher. *The Writer's Journey*. 2 ed. California: Michael Wiese Productions, 1998.

Acknowledgments

Men often say that there's this secret girl network, where we meet every month during the full moon on the top of Topanga Canyon and discuss *everything* every single man in the entire world has ever said or done.

Well, guess what—*it's true!*

Big hugs of gratitude go out to my not-so-secret girl network for sharing their stories and offering support and encouragement: Iris Levy, Laurie (*You Have to Kiss a Lot of Frogs*) Graff, Leora Skolkin-Smith, Elizabeth Gold, Tess Link, Jamie Diamond, Vicki Hoffer, Betsy Aaron, Marcie Hoffman, Caroline Rosenstone, Jessica Lee, Joanna West, Mary Garipoli, Adele Reina, Margo Perin, C. J. Golden, Susan Dunigan, Margaret McCarthy, Tina DeMarco, Kit Reuther, Ellen Kesend, Lesley Goren, Claudia Kuttner, Susan Yolen, Joy (*Housewives on Prozac*) Rose, Vicki Juditz, Janet Fitch, Tina Stephens, Christie LeBlanc, and Daphne Kalatoy. You gals rock!

And the men—ah fellas, I love you! Many thanks to (first names only, *please!*) Roberto, Frank, Devin, Richard, Ted, David, and all the members of my delicious coterie.

I curtsey to my mentor/heroes—Eric Epstein, Sy Klausner, and Richard Walter. Thanks to Werner for coming to my rescue. Thank you to Ian Kerner, PhD (*Be Honest You're Just Not That Into Him Either*) for all your generosity. Thank you to Pat Quinn for believing in me. Thank you to Susie Bright for including me in the *Best American Erotica*. And thank you to Peter Pruce—if it weren't for you, I'd have to type on the floor!

Special thanks to The Stromboli Eight and my brilliant Wesleyan students.

Norrie Epstein, I don't know you, but the day you decided to bring back Doris Langley Moore's book, *The Technique of the Love Affair,* you changed my life. You gave me my muse and I thank you.

I am in debt to the Virginia Center for the Creative Arts for granting me an International Fellowship to Oberphfalzer Kunstlerhaus where I wrote much of this book. Thank you to Stephen Dunn for the Eastern Frontier Society Fellowship. I know I said in my proposal I was working on a novel, but well, truth is, I started writing this instead—maybe it was all the wine and the soft-shell lobster!

I send out kisses to my workshop pal, Lindsay Ahl in Santa Fe, who kept me going when the going got rough.

Thank you to my brilliant, kind, and faithful agent, Julia Lord. You changed my life. Thank you to my extraordinarily wise editor, Deb Werksman of Sourcebooks.

Thank you to my talented and hard working intern, Eric—the James Dean for the new millennium.

Thank you to my Dad, for telling me about the old days, for dating my mom, for marrying her, and for surviving World War II just so that I could be born.

Thank you to my gorgeous daughter, Callan, for—well, just because.

And finally, thank you, Bill. I love you!

About the Author

Jamie Callan's fiction has appeared in *Best American Erotica*, *The Missouri Review*, *American Letters & Commentary*, and *Story*. She has received fellowships and grants from the New York State Council on the Arts, the Bread Loaf Writers Conference, and the Connecticut Commission on the Arts. She has a BA in literature from Bard College, an MFA in creative writing from Goddard College, and an MFA in screenwriting from the UCLA School of Theatre, Film, and Television. Jamie teaches writing in Wesleyan University's Graduate Liberal Studies Program.

She is married and lives in Woods Hole, Massachusetts.

You can visit Jamie at www.JamieCatCallan.com